ENDORSEMENTS

Peter Madden has a fresh new approach to preaching, which is evident in his writings. He is able, through prophetic message, to bring forward challenging insights into God's Word.

—*Dr. Steve Ryder*
Reach Out for Christ, International Ministries
Gold Coast, Australia

I was particularly impressed by Mr. Madden's interest in the revival work of Smith Wigglesworth. Since I had been a friend of Leonard Ravenhill, who prayed hours every day for revival during his lifetime, I remember that he often spoke with admiration about the heart of revival in Wigglesworth's ministry. Hopefully, this book will increase the fervor in the hearts of [Madden's] readers to emulate Wigglesworth in dying to self and living through Christ in complete surrender. Kathryn Kuhlman's testimony at the end of the book is a stirring reminder of what God can do with a totally yielded servant.

—*Betty Daffin*
Last Days Ministries

Pastor Peter Madden challenges Christians to let the power of the cross deal with the enemy within. The truth of his message has had profound effects on my life, and I know you will be impacted, too!

—*Pastor Francis Apurel*
President, Miracle Ministries
Papua, New Guinea

SMITH
WIGGLESWORTH'S

KEYS TO
POWER

SMITH WIGGLESWORTH'S

KEYS TO POWER

PETER J. MADDEN

WHITAKER
HOUSE

Whitaker House thanks the Home of Peace, Oakland, California, for providing portions of the Smith Wigglesworth material included in this book, and the Kathryn Kuhlman Foundation, Pittsburgh, Pennsylvania, for permission to use the excerpts of Kathryn Kuhlman's testimony in the epilogue.

SMITH WIGGLESWORTH'S KEYS TO POWER

(previously published as *The Keys to Wigglesworth's Power*)

ISBN-13: 978-1-60374-636-6
eBook ISBN: 978-1-60374-764-6
Printed in the United States of America
© 2000, 2013 by Whitaker House

Whitaker House
1030 Hunt Valley Circle
New Kensington, PA 15068
www.whitakerhouse.com

Library of Congress Cataloging-in-Publication Data
Madden, Peter J., 1961–
[Secret of Wigglesworth's power]
The keys to Wigglesworth's power / by Peter J. Madden.
p. cm.
Summary: "Explores specific keys in the life and ministry of Smith Wigglesworth that transformed him from an ordinary plumber into one of the most compelling healing evangelists of the twentieth century"
—Provided by publisher.
Includes bibliographical references.
ISBN-13: 978-0-88368-168-8 (trade pbk. : alk. paper)
ISBN-10: 0-88368-168-4 (trade pbk. : alk. paper)
1. Wigglesworth, Smith, 1859–1947. 2. Christian life—Pentecostal authors. I. Title.
BX8762.Z8W542 2005
289.9'4'092—dc22   2005007241

1 2 3 4 5 6 7 8 9 10 11 ῶ 20 19 18 17 16 15 14 13

DEDICATION

To my four young champions in God:
Rebekah, Jordan, Jeshua, and Haddas.

ACKNOWLEDGMENTS

Many thanks to...

The Home of Peace, Oakland, California—where I found these wonderful messages of Smith Wigglesworth.

Ray Bloomfield—who shared the "A Little Touch of Heaven" story with me and has been a great inspiration over the years.

The Pastors of Tuolumne County, California—who were my dear friends and prayer partners during the writing of this book.

The Kathryn Kuhlman Foundation, Pittsburgh, Pennsylvania—for permission to use the testimony of Kathryn Kuhlman in the epilogue.

CONTENTS

FOREWORD

I am honored to write this Foreword and commendation for my dear friend and fellow minister of the gospel, Peter Madden.

As we observe the transition from one millennium to another, I am acutely aware, as an international speaker and traveler, that we are also observing the passing of many traditional values and methodologies simply because they are considered part of the old way of doing things and hence no longer relevant. History teaches us that some things are temporal or transitional, yet other things are permanent or eternal.

In the twenty-first century, the industrial age moves aside as the information technology age moves center stage and we become more reliant upon impersonal, faceless systems rather than interrelational methods. However, contrary to contemporary opinion, God's systems have always involved men, not machines. E. M. Bounds, the great Christian author, once expressed the same idea when he said that God's methods always involve men. I do not advocate an uncompromising, inflexible, stoic resistance to change; however, in the process of change, we must take extreme care not to throw out historical values with their associated philosophy simply because they are considered old and part of yesterday's obsolete methodology. Peter Madden likewise asserts this position in this book as he profiles the life of a great evangelist of the previous century.

The lesson most learned from history is that we never seem to learn from history—and the church with its concepts is no exception to this truism. The historical path of the church and its theology is one of consistently going to extremes and falling into heresy. Constant investigation of philosophical and intellectual theories, which have proven not only unworkable but also heretical, have plagued the church's progress and consequently displayed a mentality of continual reinvention of the wheel.

Unsubstantiated and irrational claims to truth, followed by challenges and counterclaims, color the church's credibility in a hostile world that demands that the adherents of the Christian faith be accountable and in allegiance to one another. Because of the nature of the church's public profile and its condemnation of the secular lifestyle of the society in which it coexists, the world surely retains a right to demand a certain moral standard from those who espouse these ethics and pious beliefs, and who, in turn, act as the moral conscience.

> *There is no shortcut to truth or free, easy ride to revival.*

Practicality and realism are sadly lacking in contemporary (especially Western) Christian thought; truths such as humility and sacrifice are no longer words considered acceptable in a modern church setting. However, I, like Peter, have a strong conviction that God will demand no less a response from our generation than any preceding one, in that there is no shortcut to truth, and certainly no free, easy ride to revival. We will have to return to historical mainstream revival teaching to subsequently take the next dispensational step forward in godly renewal. It can only be founded on biblically based principles and precedents.

It is into this scenario of modern Christian thought that Peter has attempted to bring a balanced and somewhat traditional viewpoint of revival as seen in the life of evangelist Smith Wigglesworth. In no sense is this viewpoint obsolete; to the contrary, I consider it to be the fundamental ingredient missing in most modern revival preaching. Peter has attempted to present, as an example to us, a great evangelist who was the epitome of a preacher of power and manifestations on the one hand, and yet, balanced on the other, a man of deep consecration and self-sacrifice in his pursuit of God and divine renewal. It is for this reason I commend this book to you.

—Brian Hay
International Evangelist

Introduction:

The Legacy of Smith Wigglesworth

The Power to Heal

Quickly, he's coming!"

Word had come to this San Francisco family that a man who moved in the power of Jesus Christ to heal was walking the streets of the inner city, preaching and praying for the sick. He walked the streets, for there were so many people who wanted to hear him that he had decided this was the best way.

He wasn't far from their house now, and they struggled to get their youngest daughter down the front steps and onto the footpath, in order to join the other sick people who lined the street. As he turned the corner, they heard him speak the Word of God and found themselves riveted to every word, deeply convinced of their own sinful state, yet strangely filled with an ability to believe that they too would receive the miracle they had longed for.

One by one, as Wigglesworth's shadow passed over them, their neighbors were miraculously healed. They held their breath as he approached their own precious one. They believed now, beyond the shadow of a doubt, the message this man declared, that Jesus heals today.

As he passed her, they saw with their own eyes the *"testimony of Jesus"* (Revelation 19:10) in the healing of their loved one, as had those in Jerusalem some 1900 years earlier when the apostle Peter had walked the streets.[1]

The Power to Live in Divine Health

Dr. Lanz sprang to his feet. "Wigglesworth, why are you preaching divine health when you have false teeth?" Wigglesworth replied simply, "I will give the man five pounds who can prove that I have had any dental work done in the last fifty years."

After the meeting, Dr. Lanz, a famous Swiss dental surgeon, repented and believed as he examined the most perfect set of teeth he had ever seen in a human mouth of any age, let alone a man of eighty-one.[2]

The Power to Bring Conviction

"You convict us of sin."

The two ministers in clerical collars, traveling on a train approaching Ireland, fell to their knees and wept in conviction of sin and their own wretchedness, profoundly affected by the power that came from this small, gray-haired man, Smith Wigglesworth—a power that they knew was the reality of Jesus but that was manifested in a way they had never experienced before. From that day on, their lives were never the same.[3]

Smith Wigglesworth was a man of astounding faith who had an awesome revelation of Jesus Christ. He was a revivalist. He lived in the Spirit in a measure that was seen in very few other men or women of God in the twentieth century. In fact, he lived in the Spirit in such a measure that, in the last thirty-five years of his life, he moved out of the natural order and lived completely in the supernatural realm, and multitudes were saved, healed, delivered, and reconciled wherever he went.

The unique phenomenon that was Wigglesworth has inspired millions, even since his death in 1947, and as yet we have not seen many approach the standard and level of life in the Spirit to which he attained. However, in the closing stages of this age, as we approach the imminent return of our Lord and Savior Jesus Christ, I believe that God is calling forth an army that will walk in the same standard of life in the Spirit, God's "end-times army." This army will go out and reap the great end-times harvest, which must be reaped before His return.

Is There Only One "Wigglesworth" in a Generation?

There are some who would say, "There is only one Wigglesworth in a generation, and the appearance of a special one like him is totally dependent on God's sovereignly choosing to raise him up." But I must differ from this opinion, for I believe with all my heart that God would not have given us this standard and written us this "living letter" (see 2 Corinthians 3:3) through his life, unless He wanted us to know that the standard of Wigglesworth's walk in the Spirit is possible and is a mark toward which we are to press.

The Essence of Revival

Jesus said, "Ask, and it will be given to you; seek, and you will find; knock, and it will be opened to you" (Matthew 7:7). But we must know what we are to seek and ask for, and I find in Wigglesworth a mark for which to seek and ask.

In our pursuit of God's fullness, and as we ask Him to direct us in our study of the life and messages of this man of God; in our desire to read and analyze this

Wigglesworth knew the reality of being "crucified with Christ."

"letter" to find the reason for the awesome power of God that flowed like a great river through his life, we must understand that the degree to which Wigglesworth was filled with the Spirit was directly related to the degree to which he knew the reality of being *"crucified with Christ"* (Galatians 2:20). This was the essence of revival in his life. We see the glorious power of the cross in both his life and his messages. This was the very foundation of the secret of God's power in Wigglesworth, and it is the foundation for the coming revival to which we are called to be a part.

The Bride and the Army

God is searching the earth for an army! In the final stages of this age, He is calling forth His army—bold, tough, and relentless in their battle against *"the beast, the kings of the earth, and their armies"* (Revelation 19:19). He is also calling forth His bride—precious, pure, and lovely (verses 7–8). We see both being called forth by many of God's prophets and teachers worldwide, and we must realize that they are one and the same. Both are the true church. Both are the remnant. Both are the *"sons of the living God"* (Romans 9:26).

There is a great, great harvest to be reaped in these last of the last days, and indeed *"the fields…are already white for harvest!"* (John 4:35). However, *"unless a grain of wheat falls into the ground and dies, it remains alone; but if it dies, it produces much grain"* (John 12:24).

> *Many miss the fullness of revival power by seeking only the cross or the Holy Spirit, but not both.*

In the church today, the evangelicals seek a Wesley- and Whitefield-type revival, a Jonathan Edwards-type awakening, such as God brought in the 1700s, or a revival like the kind Charles Finney was used by God to bring in the 1800s. Yet, sadly, even though it is absolutely essential that we seek this type of revival—for it is revival based on repentance and the cross—evangelicals miss the power of the Holy Spirit.

On the other hand, Pentecostals and charismatics seek a revival of power, with great signs, wonders, and the outpouring of the Holy Spirit in the gifts of the miraculous and the prophetic. Yet, sadly, many Pentecostals miss the fullness and the beauty of the message of the cross.

The Union of Calvary and Pentecost

The great end-times revival will not come until we see a marriage of both. It will not come until we see the coming together of both Calvary and Pentecost, of the cross and the power, of death to self and the radical life displayed in the Acts of the Apostles. For as the first great revival did not come without both, neither will the last. Wigglesworth embodied this union,

Wigglesworth embodied the union of the cross and power.

the union of the cross and power. The more I read of the Wigglesworth "epistle," the more I see this, and the more I desire the awesome place of this union that he found in Christ.

Many will read this book because of the miracles and the signs and wonders that occurred in Wigglesworth's ministry. My prayer is that they will find the cross, too. I also pray that Pentecostals and charismatics who read this book will share it with their evangelical friends, so that they may read it and, seeing the cross, find the power.

Wanted: Laborers for the Harvest

Therefore pray the Lord of the harvest to send out laborers into His harvest. (Matthew 9:38)

My prayer is that this book may be part of the process of "sending out" these laborers, this army, by challenging those called by God

> *The principles that marked Wigglesworth's life need to become personal realities for us.*

to take up the cross to the measure that Smith Wigglesworth did, so that they may be able to claim the "mantle" that was given to him (see 1 Kings 19:19–21; 2 Kings 2:9–15), and, in so doing, reap the great end-times harvest.

If you have not read my first book, *The Wigglesworth Standard*,[4] I strongly urge you to do so. It lays the foundation for us to effectively enter a fuller understanding and personal application of the "Wigglesworth epistle" and to attain to the amazing life in the Spirit to which he attained. The awesome principles that we discover in Wigglesworth's life and messages, the mark of his life that we can look toward and aim for—which is, to a degree, *"the mark for the prize of the high calling of God in Christ Jesus"* (Philippians 3:14 KJV)—the great challenges that were laid down in *The Wigglesworth Standard*: all these must become life realities to us and not just more head knowledge.

So, my friends, as I wrote in *The Wigglesworth Standard*,

> You have heard the call. You have felt the challenge. You have sensed the thrill of the potential that is within you....You can be *"filled with God"* just as Wigglesworth was. You can be a *"flame of fire"* in God's "end-times army."[5]

Now, through the additional keys to his life and ministry that are set forth in this book, let us move forward in furthering this goal!

—*Peter J. Madden*

For to this you were called, because Christ also suffered for us, leaving us an example, that you should follow His steps. (1 Peter 2:21)

Be ye followers after me, even as I also am of Christ. (1 Corinthians 11:1 KJV)

PART 1:

PASSING THE MANTLE

PASSING THE MANTLE

All of Self – None of God
Some of Self – Some of God
None of Self – All of God[1]

It was a spring day in early March 1947. Smith Wigglesworth sat at a table in the small stone cottage in Bradford, Yorkshire, Northern England, that was his home, conversing with a young friend named Albert Hibbert. As they talked of the things of God, Wigglesworth, with tears in his eyes, exhorted his friend to move on in the things of the Spirit. His great desire was to "pass the mantle" and to see others rise up and be great for God—to see others go and draw this lost world to Christ.

"When are you going to move into a realm that you have not yet touched and get going for God?" he asked.[2]

Wigglesworth's life had been one of drawing men to Christ. More than anything else, he was a soulwinner. He burned with a passion for souls, with a tremendous compassion for the sick and hurting, and an immense desire to be a reflection of Jesus to a lost and dying world.

He lived to reveal the fullness of Christ to as many people as he could, and he yearned to draw Christians into new realms in God, to new heights in the Spirit, and into a "greater sphere of usefulness for His glory." He had experienced so much of God all across the globe, and he very much wanted to pass on his experience of God to others.

Although he had spent many years traveling the world, he was now back in Bradford, the town that had been his home for most of his life. He had spent so many wonderful years there with Polly, his evangelist wife, whom he loved with an enormous passion, and over whom he had wept bitterly at the time of her death, as she told him that the Lord wanted her.

> *"When are you going to move into a realm that you have not yet touched and get going for God?"*

This was the town where he had raised his children and where he had accommodated and shown hospitality to hundreds over the years who were in the Lord's work. It was where Wigglesworth himself had been given a sentence of death by a doctor many years before; but he had found God's healing power and had proved God over modern medicine.

He was an old man now, as far as his years went; however, he was far from having the symptoms of age that others of similar years had, for he had proven the reality of both Scripture and the Spirit of God in his own body:

> *But if the Spirit of Him who raised Jesus from the dead dwells in you, He who raised Christ from the dead will also give life to your mortal bodies through His Spirit who dwells in you.*
>
> (Romans 8:11)

"I am an old man, eighty-seven years of age," he told Hibbert. "I may not look it; I certainly don't feel it. But you cannot argue with the birth certificate, and it tells me I am eighty-seven. So I have to accept it, regardless of how I feel about it."[3]

Wigglesworth's Definition of Success

Smith Wigglesworth had said before, more than once, that he did not regret at all the life he had lived. On this occasion, though, his heart was breaking as he pondered the invitations he had received that morning from all over the world, for they meant to him failure, not success.

He told Hibbert, "Today in my mail I had an invitation to Australia, one to India and Ceylon, and one to America. People have their eyes on me." "Then," Hibbert recalled, "he sobbed as if his heart would break. 'Poor Wigglesworth,' he weeped. 'What a failure to think that people have their eyes on me. God will never give His glory to another! He will take me from the scene!'"[4]

The following Saturday, in the vestry of a nearby church, as he was speaking with a friend before a funeral service, Wigglesworth was "taken from the scene." One moment he was in full health, talking calmly, and the next he was gone into the presence of his Lord.

Wigglesworth lived to reveal the fullness of Christ to as many people as he could.

The realm in which he had lived during the last thirty-five years of his life was one where the Holy Spirit had brought to death, burned up, all of the man "Wigglesworth." Multitudes around the world had seen only Jesus when they looked at him. This was the essence of revival and the secret of the power in his life; it was his heart's greatest desire that he would not be seen, but that he would bear only the *"testimony of Jesus"* (Revelation 19:10), so that Jesus alone would be seen. To this man who had come to know God so intimately, success was when people could see Jesus in his life and ministry. Failure, on the other hand, was when they had their focus on him and his ministry. Knowing that "God will never give His glory to another" (see Isaiah 42:8), letters like the ones he received that morning broke his heart.

Living As the "New Man"

Wigglesworth had found the most glorious life available to anyone. He had found the place of fully living as the *"new man"* (Ephesians 4:24), which is also called the *"inner man"* (Ephesians 3:16), living completely in the born-again nature.

This life, and the entering into of this life, is the subject and prophetic message of this book. Wigglesworth did not find it overnight. In fact, it was his overwhelming desire, his grand passion, for many, many years. Yet he saw it and sought it and prayed for it, and he believed God for it until he found its fullness in his life. It is the prophetic message in both his life and his teaching that rings out clearly to anyone *"who has an ear [to] hear"* (Revelation 2:7).

The Last Recorded Conversation

It is very important to note that the last recorded conversation of Smith Wigglesworth exemplified this message. The main cry of his spirit was that Jesus be seen and that people might not see him but Christ. It contained both exhortation and the cry that Jesus be seen through him.

Just as Wigglesworth challenged Albert Hibbert on that day a week before he died, I believe this is his challenge to all of us who aspire to reach the greater realms: "When are you going to move into a realm that you have not yet touched and get going for God?"

The Cord of Three Strands: The Cross, the Stone, and the Fire

The process that had brought about the reality of the *"new man"* in his life—the process of coming into the fullness of bearing the *"testimony of Jesus"* (Revelation 19:10), of being clothed with His power, of the removal of the natural Smith, and of having all that was of self and the flesh brought to nothing—was a fascinating and wonderful journey.

It was the journey of the cross, the stone, and the fire! And it is a pilgrimage to which we are all called.

First, the journey involves voluntarily choosing to surrender to the cross and the death of self thereon:

> *I have been crucified with Christ; it is no longer I who live, but Christ lives in me; and the life which I now live in the flesh I live by faith in the Son of God, who loved me and gave Himself for me.*
> (Galatians 2:20)

Second, the journey means being broken by falling on the Cornerstone:

> *Have you never read in the Scriptures: "The stone which the builders rejected has become the chief cornerstone. This was the Lord's doing, and it is marvelous in our eyes"?…And whoever falls on this stone will be broken; but on whomever it falls, it will grind him to powder.*
> (Matthew 21:42, 44)

Third, the journey involves the purification and tempering of your faith by the Holy Spirit's refining fire:

> *That the trial of your faith, being much more precious than of gold that perisheth, though it be tried with fire, might be found unto praise and honour and glory at the appearing of Jesus Christ.*
> (1 Peter 1:7 KJV)

Though my primary concern in this book is the *"message of the cross"* (1 Corinthians 1:18), you will also find references to the stone and the fire, to brokenness and the trial of faith, for they are a *"cord of three strands"* (Ecclesiastes 4:12 NASB) that cannot be separated. Further, they are themes that occur consistently throughout Wigglesworth's teachings.

A Prophetic Letter for the Church

My first book, *The Wigglesworth Standard*, begins with these words:

Clearly you are an epistle of Christ…written not with ink but by the Spirit of the living God, not on tablets of stone but on tablets of flesh, that is, of the heart. (2 Corinthians 3:3)

Smith Wigglesworth constantly preached this truth, which was definitely exhibited by his own life. He was truly a living *"epistle of Christ."* As we look at the heart and message of this great man of faith, we learn some wonderful lessons and read some great and mighty things on the pages of his life.

The very first time I heard of Smith Wigglesworth, the Holy Spirit stirred within me and said, "I have a special message for you, written on the life and testimony of this man, which will affect your whole life and ministry. Go and learn about him!"[5]

I believe that Wigglesworth is a prophetic *"epistle"* to the church today, just as he was a living letter to the early-twentieth-century church. He is a prophetic living letter, and the message that the Holy Spirit told me He had for me, which is written on Wigglesworth's life and testimony, is for the end-times church. This prophetic message has its foundation in the true understanding of the three strands of the scarlet cord—the cross, the stone, and the fire—and the ramifications for several different theological viewpoints that are prevalent in the church today. This will become clearer as the book develops, but here I will briefly mention one of these theological issues, which is often a major issue in the church.

There is much controversy in the church worldwide concerning the doctrine of the rapture, or the "catching away" of the church to be with Christ (see 1 Thessalonians 4:16–17), and the great tribulation (see, for example, Matthew 24:4–31; Revelation 7:13–14). Some believe that the church will be raptured into heaven before the tribulation, some believe it will be raptured during the tribulation, and some believe it will be raptured after the tribulation. These three beliefs are usually referred to as the pre-tribulation (pre-trib), mid-tribulation (mid-trib), and post-tribulation (post-trib) views, respectively.

Behind the Divergent Viewpoints:
A Unifying Message

I will not enter into the tribulation controversy in this book except to say that, having considered all three views, I have seen that behind all the deep scriptural, numerical, and typological studies concerning each view is the message of the three-strand cord of the cross, the stone, and the fire and its work in the Christian's life. You may ask, In what way?

> *Our spiritual condition does not always match our spiritual position in Christ.*

The pre-tribulation view is held primarily by those who advocate a theology that comes from a positional base. This has been an important move of God over the past thirty years in teaching the church who we are in Christ—our position and our authority in Him. However, in many cases, teachers of this positional view have carried certain truths too far, beyond an appropriate balance, by not keeping them in perspective with other important truths.

Smith Wigglesworth, who is considered one of the greatest "apostles of faith" of the twentieth century, preached positional truths balanced with an emphasis on God's use of the cross, the stone, and the fire to bring about the breaking and purification in our lives that is necessary regarding our spiritual condition—for our condition does not always match our position in Christ.

I have found it very interesting that many of the valid, major prophetic ministries whose messages I have heard tend toward the mid-trib or post-trib views. This is a very important observation because the prophets of God are called to speak to the condition of the church while the teachers are called to speak about the position of the church in Christ.

Those who advocate the post-trib view see the need for the purification of the church; they base their view on the idea that this purification of a very carnal church will come about through the stone of brokenness and the fire of trial in the tribulation. Put very simply:

Teachers	Prophets
See the church's position	See the church's condition
Tend toward a pre-trib belief	Tend toward post-trib or mid-trib beliefs

Whether you hold to a pre-, mid-, or post-trib position, I am sure you will agree that, without any doubt, God wants the best for His church and that Jesus is coming back for a purified church, a bride without spot or blemish. (See Ephesians 5:27.) So the question becomes, How is He going to purify His bride from the rampant carnality that so much of the church exhibits today?

This purification must occur either through purging by the fire of trial and the stone of breaking or through a deep work of prophetic revival rooted in the cross, in order to strip away the carnality of the twenty-first century church. I believe that this revival will come through prophetic teaching and preaching ministries such as that of Smith Wigglesworth, whose teaching took into account both our position and our condition. This revival of the power of the cross provides the only alternative to purification through an extreme work of the stone and the fire, for it is God's path to circumventing some of the trials, suffering, and breaking in our lives. Although there will always be an element of the stone and the fire in our lives, our need for it will be in counterbalance to the depth of the work of the cross that we embrace.

A deep work of prophetic revival, rooted in the cross, can strip away the carnality that is rampant in the church today.

There are some who teach that purification can come about only through the suffering that we experience in life, yet this negates the scriptural teaching on the power of the cross to deliver and set us free as we willingly deny ourselves and surrender our lives to God. (See, for example, Matthew 16:24; Galatians 6:14.)

Alternately, there are those who teach that suffering is not of God, and that, through the application of certain principles, it can be avoided. However, this negates both the teaching of Scripture and the biblical and historical evidence of God's use of the stone and the fire in all the men and women whom He has greatly used. (See, for example, Genesis 32:24–31; Romans 5:3–5; Romans 8:18; Hebrews 5:7–8; James 5:10, 13.)

> *Embracing the cross and self-denial is God's alternative to some of the trials and breaking in our lives.*

We must see that all three strands of the three-strand cord will be with us until we *"meet the Lord in the air"* (1 Thessalonians 4:17). However, we must also hear God's call to the most powerful and important strand—the call to the cross! I believe that there is a great end-times revival of purification and the perfecting in *agape* love coming to the church worldwide, and it is a revival based in the message of the cross. It is coming to those who will embrace it and open their ears to a message of self-denial that is too often lost to us in our desire for an easy way through life.

Wigglesworth's message was this very message of faith combined with the call to the cross, which is the prophetic message that this book declares. If you are reading this book in search of attaining greater realms in God and the power that flowed like a river through Wigglesworth's life, then you will hear it.

The Questions That Keep Wigglesworth's Ministry Alive

The thing about Smith Wigglesworth that has intrigued people all over the world, more than anything else, is the power of God that flowed through him—the extraordinary power that convicted people of sin, healed the sick, and revealed the marvelous sovereignty of God in granting him divine health in the major battles against sickness he had in his own life. The great questions that have kept the intense interest in him alive to hungry hearts are these:

1. What was this immense power and anointing?

2. How can we realize it for ourselves?

Many have copied his style, thinking that this might give them power, but to no avail. Many have put it down to gifting, thinking that he had incredible gifts and that the anointing was the secret of his power; they have prayed in vain for years that God would give them the same gifts. But as I have studied and continue to study Wigglesworth, I have seen that it was not solely either style or gifts, but rather that Wigglesworth found the depth of the power of the cross combined with the power of Pentecost.

The secret of his anointing was an unshakeable faith, the rock of brokenness, and the fire of the Holy Spirit. But the central, supreme factor in his life, upon which these were based, was the depth of the outworking of the cross in his life. It was that factor that removed Wigglesworth (the natural man) from view, so that only the new man, formed by God and joined intimately with Him, could be seen.

> *The secret to a powerful anointing is the depth of the outworking of the cross in your life.*

How can we realize it for ourselves? So then, in asking this second question, the only answer can be: through seeking the same faith and depth of revelation and manifestation of the nature of Christ that Wigglesworth had and, in so doing, seeking the level of the infilling of the Holy Spirit that he experienced.

The examples of the legacy of Wigglesworth's life and ministry that are included at the beginning of this book demonstrate very clearly the power that prevailed in his life: the power that brought phenomenal healing to the sick, the power that brought about divine health in his own body, and the power that brought conviction of sin and real repentance to those around him without a word being spoken by him.

However, we must not see Wigglesworth's ministry as just power. It was what the book of Revelation calls *"the testimony of Jesus"* (Revelation 19:10). To walk in the power that Wigglesworth walked in is to live in the fullness of the *"inner man"* (Ephesians 3:16). It is to bear witness to the *"testimony of Jesus,"* which only the *"new man"* (Ephesians 4:24) is able to bear witness to. In this, we see that our desire to be filled with God's power must be married to both a passion for Christlikeness and a longing that only Christ will be seen in us—as indeed Wigglesworth had—or else we will fail.

"God Spoke to Me"

One of the greatest events in Wigglesworth's life happened while he was staying at the home of the Stormont family in England. It wasn't a spectacular miracle or a seemingly phenomenal event in comparison with what many consider to be phenomenal events, yet it was one of the most significant experiences that Wigglesworth had.

Wigglesworth told George Stormont that God had spoken to him.

It might seem odd that this would have affected Wigglesworth in such a manner because Jesus spoke to him every day. But somehow this time was different and special. George Stormont gave this firsthand account of the incident in his book, *Wigglesworth: A Man Who Walked with God*:

> When Smith Wigglesworth stayed in our home once, he came down early one morning and told me, "God spoke to me on your bed."
>
> "What did He say?" I asked.
>
> "He said, 'Wigglesworth, I am going to burn you all up, until there is no more Wigglesworth, only Jesus.'"

Standing at the foot of our stairs, he raised his hands to heaven, and with tears running down his cheeks, he cried, "O, God, come and do it! I don't want them to see me anymore—only Jesus!"[6]

This was his message; this was his cry. This was the prophetic work that God did in him, and that He must do in all of us, so that we all may be living letters to a dying world. This was the secret of Wigglesworth's power. This is the essence of revival.

You are an epistle of Christ, ministered by us, written not with ink but by the Spirit of the living God, not on tablets of stone but on tablets of flesh, that is, of the heart.

(2 Corinthians 3:3)

PART 2:

EPISTLES OF CHRIST

EPISTLES OF CHRIST

I n the first part of this book, we have seen how Smith Wigglesworth was a living letter—an epistle of Christ written to the entire world— in the pages of which the life and nature of Christ Himself could be seen. The key to being a living letter is to put to death the carnal man or the "natural order," as Wigglesworth so often quaintly expressed it, and to live in surrender to the power of the cross.

Through one of Smith Wiggleworth's sermons, "Epistles of Christ, Manifesting Forth His Glory," we can read in Wigglesworth's own words the powerful message of what it means to be a living letter and to be able to impact the world around us. Following this meaningful sermon, I will draw out some specific keys from this teaching that illustrate the themes we are exploring from Wigglesworth's life and how they apply to us personally.

EPISTLES OF CHRIST, MANIFESTING FORTH HIS GLORY

A Message by Smith Wigglesworth

I want to read to you this morning the entire third chapter of 2 Corinthians:

Do we begin again to commend ourselves? Or do we need, as some others, epistles of commendation to you or letters of commendation from you? You are our epistle written in our hearts, known and read by all men; clearly you are an epistle of Christ, ministered by us, written not with ink but by the Spirit of the living God, not on tablets of stone but on tablets of flesh, that is, of the heart. And we have such trust through Christ toward God. Not that we are sufficient of ourselves to think of anything as being from ourselves, but our sufficiency is from God, who also made us sufficient as ministers of the new covenant, not of the letter but of the Spirit; for the letter kills, but the Spirit gives life. But if the ministry of death, written and engraved on stones, was glorious, so that the children of Israel could not look steadily at the face of Moses because of the glory of his countenance, which glory was passing away, how will the ministry of the Spirit not be more glorious? For if the ministry of condemnation had glory, the ministry of righteousness exceeds much more in glory. For even what was made glorious had no glory in this respect, because of the glory that excels. For if what is passing away was glorious, what remains is much more glorious. Therefore, since we have such hope, we use great boldness of speech; unlike Moses, who put a veil over his face so that the children of Israel could not look steadily at the end of what was passing away. But their minds were blinded. For until this day the same veil remains unlifted in the reading of the Old Testament, because the veil is taken away in Christ. But even to this day, when Moses is read, a veil lies on their heart. Nevertheless when one turns to the Lord, the veil is taken away. Now the Lord is the Spirit; and where the Spirit of the Lord is, there is liberty. But we all, with unveiled face, beholding as in a mirror the glory of the Lord, are being transformed into the same image from glory to glory, just as by the Spirit of the Lord.

(2 Corinthians 3)

We have in this chapter one of those high-water marks of the very deep things of God in the Spirit. I believe that God will reveal to us these truths as our hearts are open and receptive to the Spirit's leadings.

But do not let anyone think that he will receive anything from the Lord except along the lines of spiritual revelation, for there is nothing that will profit you except what denounces or brings to death the natural order, so that the supernatural plan of God may be revealed in you.

The Lord of Hosts encamps around us this morning with songs of deliverance (see Psalm 34:7), so that we may see the glories of His grace in a new way. For God has not brought us into *"cunningly devised fables"* (2 Peter 1:16), but, in these days, He is rolling away the mist and clouds so that we may understand the mind and will of God.

If we are going to get the best that God has for us, there must be a spiritual desire, an open ear, an understanding heart. The "veil" must be lifted. We must see the Lord glorified in the midst of us. We must clearly see that we are not going to be able to understand these mysteries that God is unfolding except along the lines of being filled with the Spirit.

We must see that God has nothing for us along the old lines. The new plan, the new revelation, the new victories are before us. All carnal things, evil powers, and *"spiritual wickedness in high places"* (Ephesians 6:12 KJV) must be dethroned.

Let us consider the Word, which is so beautiful and so expressive:

You are our epistle written in our hearts, known and read by all men; clearly you are an epistle of Christ, ministered by us, written not with ink but by the Spirit of the living God, not on tablets of stone but on tablets of flesh, that is, of the heart.

(2 Corinthians 3:2–3)

What an ideal position, that now the sons of God are being manifested; now the glory is being seen; now the work is becoming an expressed purpose in life until the old life has ceased in them. How truly this position was shown forth in the life of Paul when he said,

I have been crucified with Christ; it is no longer I who live, but Christ lives in me; and the life which I now live in the flesh I live by faith in the Son of God, who loved me and gave Himself for me.

(Galatians 2:20)

Beloved, God would have us see that no man is perfected along any lines except as the living Word abides in him. Jesus Christ is the express image of God (see Hebrews 1:3), and the Word is the only factor that works in you and brings forth these glories of identification between you and Christ.

We may begin at Genesis, going right through the Pentateuch and the other Scriptures, and be able to recite them, but unless there is the living factor within us, they will be a dead letter. *"The letter kills, but the Spirit gives life"* (2 Corinthians 3:6).

We do not know how to pray, except as the Spirit prays through us. The Spirit always brings to us the mind of God. He brings forth all your cries and all your needs; He takes the Word of God, and brings your heart, mind, and soul, with all their needs, into the presence of God. The Spirit prays according to the will of God. (See Romans 8:26–27.)

No man is able to speak and bring forth the deep things of God out of his own mind. The following Scripture rightly divides the Word of Truth (see 2 Timothy 2:15):

> *Clearly you are an epistle of Christ, ministered by us, written not with ink but by the Spirit of the living God, not on tablets of stone but on tablets of flesh, that is, of the heart.* (2 Corinthians 3:3)

May God help us to understand this, for it is out of the heart that all things proceed. (See Matthew 12:34.) When we have entered in with God into the mind of the Spirit, we have found that God enraptures our hearts. When I speak about the *"tablets of flesh, that is, of the heart"* (2 Corinthians 3:3), I mean the inward life.

Nothing is as sweet to me as to know that the heart yearns with compassion. Eyes may see, ears may hear, but you may be immovable along the lines of love and compassion unless you have an inward cry where *"deep calls unto deep"* (Psalm 42:7). When God gets into the depths of our hearts, He purifies every intention of our thoughts, and fills us with His own joy.

When Moses received the tablets of stone on which the commandments were written, God caused his face to shine with great joy. (See

Exodus 34:29.) Deeper than that, more wonderful than that, are His commandments written in our hearts, the deep movings of eternity rolling in and bringing God in! Oh, beloved, may our God, the Holy Spirit, have His way today in thus unfolding to us the grandeurs of Christ's glory.

> *And we have such trust through Christ toward God. Not that we are*
> *sufficient of ourselves to think of anything as being from ourselves, but*
> *our sufficiency is from God.* (2 Corinthians 3:4–5)

Ah, it is lovely! Those verses are all too deep to pass over. That is the height of exaltation, which is so different from human exaltation.

> *We need to get to a place where we are beyond trusting in ourselves.*

Beloved ones, there is so much failure in self-assurances. We must never rest upon anything in the human. Our trust is in God, and God brings us into victory. When we have no confidence in ourselves, then our whole trust rests upon the authority of the mighty God.

He has promised to be with us at all times (see Hebrews 13:5), to make the path straight (see Isaiah 42:16), and to make all the mountains into roads. (See Isaiah 49:11.) Our confidence can be fixed only on the One who never fails, the One who knows the end from the beginning. The day and the night are alike to the man who rests completely in the will of God (see Psalm 139:12), knowing that *"all things work together for good to those who love God"* (Romans 8:28).

> [God] *also made us sufficient as ministers of the new covenant, not*
> *of the letter but of the Spirit; for the letter kills, but the Spirit gives*
> *life. But if the ministry of death, written and engraved on stones, was*
> *glorious, so that the children of Israel could not look steadily at the*
> *face of Moses because of the glory of his countenance, which glory*
> *was passing away, how will the ministry of the Spirit not be more*
> *glorious? For if the ministry of condemnation had glory, the ministry*
> *of righteousness exceeds much more in glory.*
> (2 Corinthians 3:6–9)

We cannot define, separate, or deeply investigate and unfold this holy plan of God unless we have the life of God, the thought of God, the Spirit of God, and the revelation of God. The Word of Truth is pure, spiritual, and divine. The people who are spiritual can only be fed on spiritual food.

The message must be directly from heaven, red-hot, burning, living. It must be truly "Thus says the Lord," because you will speak only as the Spirit gives you utterance (see Acts 2:4), and thus you will always be giving forth fresh revelation. Whatever you say will be fruitful, elevating the mind, lifting the people, and all the people will want more.

In John's gospel, the Lord Jesus said that He did not speak or act on His own authority:

The words that I speak to you I do not speak on My own authority; but the Father who dwells in Me does the works.   (John 14:10)

We must know that the baptism of the Holy Spirit immerses us into an intensity of zeal, into the likeness of Jesus, to make us into pure metal, so hot for God that it travels like oil from vessel to vessel.

This divine life of the Spirit will let us see that we have ceased from ourselves, and that God has begun His work in us. There is not a natural thought that can be of any use here in this meeting. The natural life has to die completely, because there is no other plan for the baptized soul except to be *"dead indeed to sin"* (Romans 6:11).

We must live in the Spirit; we must realize all the time that we are living in that same ideal of our Master, in season and out of season (see 2 Timothy 4:2), always beholding the face of our Lord Jesus. Old things are done away with:

For even what was made glorious had no glory in this respect, because of the glory that excels. For if what is passing away was glorious, what remains is much more glorious.   (2 Corinthians 3:10–11)

Thank God that the very doing away of the old law fixes His commandments in our hearts more deeply than ever. For out of the depths we cry to God, and in the depths He has cast out uncleanness and revealed His righteousness within. May God lead us all, every step in His divine life.

––––––––––––––––––––

Wigglesworth's messages hold so much for us today. We need to look closely at what he is saying in this sermon and how it applies to us personally. To do this, we will look at some of the major points in his message.

KEY #1

A MESSAGE DIRECTLY FROM HEAVEN

The message must be directly from heaven, red-hot, burning, living. It must be truly "Thus says the Lord," because you will speak only as the Spirit gives you utterance (see Acts 2:4), and thus you will always be giving forth fresh revelation. Whatever you say will be fruitful, elevating the mind, lifting the people, and all the people will want more.

In John's gospel, the Lord Jesus said that He did not speak or act on His own authority: *"The words that I speak to you I do not speak on My own authority; but the Father who dwells in Me does the works"* (John 14:10). We must know that the baptism of the Holy Spirit immerses us into an intensity of zeal, into the likeness of Jesus, to make us into pure metal, so hot for God that it travels like oil from vessel to vessel.

This divine life of the Spirit will let us see that we have ceased from ourselves, and that God has begun His work in us. There is not a natural thought that can be of any use here in this meeting. The natural life has to die completely, because there is no other plan for the baptized soul except to be *"dead indeed to sin"* (Romans 6:11).

The tapestry of the concepts of the cross—of the replacement of our life with the divine life, of the baptism of the Holy Spirit immersing us fully into the likeness of Jesus, of the outflow of God's power through us, and of speaking the very message of heaven—is woven very beautifully throughout most of Wigglesworth's messages, but perhaps nowhere is it expressed more succinctly than in this message.

I speak of a tapestry, for that is precisely what it is. A tapestry with each element entwined totally with the others. A tapestry woven to the forming of a new garment. A tapestry that Wigglesworth prophetically calls us to "put on," so that we may be clothed with the glory of heaven, with *the testimony of Jesus* [which] *is the spirit of prophecy*" (Revelation 19:10). It is a garment that we have seen a number of men and women wear throughout the

> *Wigglesworth "inoculated" people with faith.*

course of history; it is the garment of the revivalist; it is the garment of the bride of Christ; it is the garment of the "army of the crucified."

Louis Pethrus, the pastor of Stockholm's huge Pentecostal church, said that when Wigglesworth preached, he would "inoculate" the congregation with faith. Bill Hacking, author of *Smith Wigglesworth Remembered*, wrote of his preaching, "One sentence sometimes was like a sermon, capable of changing the course of your life."[1] Not only in the pulpit, but also in private, his words had an awesome power in people's lives. Albert Hibbert, who wrote *Smith Wigglesworth: The Secret of His Power*, and who was a close personal friend of Wigglesworth's, said of him,

> One was never the same after having had personal fellowship with Smith Wigglesworth. That which he deposited within a person's spirit was beyond explanation. One could only understand this by experiencing it himself.[2]

As with every great revivalist, Smith Wigglesworth's message, in and out of the pulpit, was positively "directly from heaven, red-hot, burning, living." It was "truly 'Thus says the Lord.'" He spoke only as God gave him the utterance (see Ephesians 6:19), and therefore always gave forth "fresh revelation." It was "fruitful, elevating the mind, lifting the people," and all the people wanted more.

Red-Hot Preaching

The phenomenon of preaching "directly from heaven, red-hot, burning, living" is a reality that has been seen in certain men and women throughout history. These were the great revivalists. These were people who had a deep experience with Christ and the power of the cross and who literally became a direct connection from heaven to earth, from God to man. These were men and women who had stepped into a realm beyond human ability; they had stepped into the supernatural, stepped beyond themselves and into the power of the "*inner man*" (Ephesians 3:16).

These men and women also brought people into experiential truth. The difference between experiential knowledge and head knowledge is illustrated in Ephesians 3:19: "*To know [ginosko] the love of Christ which passes knowledge [gnosis]; that you may be filled with all the fullness of God.*" In the Greek, the word for experiential knowing is *ginosko*. It is a knowing that surpasses knowledge, or *gnosis*.

There are many examples throughout history of revivalists who preached "directly from heaven" and brought people into the experiential truth and knowledge of God.

The Apostle Peter

His hearers were "*cut to the heart*" (Acts 2:37).

Francis of Assisi (twelfth century)

"His words were like fire, piercing the heart."[3]

Savonarola (fifteenth century)

When people listened to Savonarola's messages,

their "eyes glazed with terror...tears gushed from their eyes; they beat their breasts and cried to God for mercy."

One famous scholar...said of him, "the mere sound of Savonarola's voice was as a clap of doom; a cold shiver ran through the marrow of his bones; the hairs of his head stood on end as he listened." Another tells how his sermons caused "such terror and alarm, such sobbing and tears that people passed through the streets...more dead than alive."[4]

George Whitefield (eighteenth century)

On the occasion of George Whitefield's first sermon, at the age of twenty-one, the presiding bishop reported that fifteen people were "driven mad."[5] After returning to England following a year in America working in an orphanage, and finding the Anglican churches closed to his radical "message from heaven," he turned to a group of miners as they came out of the coal pits.[6] As he preached, great "white gutters" appeared on the miners' blackened faces from their tears rolling down their sooty cheecks as God spoke directly into their hearts.[7]

Soon afterward, he went out to preach to them again, but there weren't two hundred there to hear—there were two thousand! Soon after that, there were four thousand, then ten thousand, fourteen thousand, twenty thousand, and on up to crowds as large as thirty thousand. Thousands would come at six o'clock in the morning in the middle of winter, standing in the snow to be charged by a message that was "red-hot, burning, living."[8]

He met men face to face, like one who had a message from God to them, "I have come here to speak to you about your soul."[9]

***

He preached like a lion. His sermons were life and fire; you must listen whether you like it or not. There was a holy violence about him which firmly took your attention by storm.[10]

***

[One convert confessed,] I came to hear you with a pocket full of stones to break your head, but your sermon got the better of me, and God broke my heart.[11]

As one who knew that his message was "directly from heaven, red-hot, burning, living,…truly, 'Thus saith the Lord,'" he said, "I have not come in my own name. No! I have come in the name of the Lord of hosts and I must and will be heard!"[12]

Jonathan Edwards (eighteenth century)

When Edwards preached his sermon "Sinners in the Hands of an Angry God," "people screamed aloud, clutched the backs of pews and the stone pillars of the church, lest the ground open and swallow them alive into hell!"[13]

Gilbert Tennant (Edwards' associate)

Regarding Tennant's ministry in Lyme, Connecticut,

Many had their countenances changed; their thoughts seemed to trouble them, so that their loins were loosed and their knees smote one against the other. Great numbers cried aloud in the anguish of their souls. Several stout men fell as though a cannon had been discharged and a ball made its way through their hearts.[14]

Charles Finney (eighteenth century)

When he opened his mouth he was aiming a gun. When he spoke bombardment began.[15]

These were the great revivalists. These were among those who found the secret of divine life in the Spirit, of "ceasing from themselves," and of speaking "directly from heaven, red-hot, burning, living" prophetic messages. God is looking for others who will do the same.

KEY #2

DEEP CALLS TO DEEP

May God help us to understand this, for it is out of the heart that all things proceed. (See Matthew 12:34.) When we have entered in with God into the mind of the Spirit, we have found that God enraptures our hearts. When I speak about the *"tablets of flesh, that is, of the heart"* (2 Corinthians 3:3), I mean the inward life.

Nothing is as sweet to me as to know that the heart yearns with compassion. Eyes may see, ears may hear, but you may be immovable along the lines of love and compassion unless you have an inward cry where *"deep calls unto deep"* (Psalm 42:7). When God gets into the depths of our hearts, He purifies every intention of our thoughts, and fills us with His own joy.

Wigglesworth spoke "red-hot, burning, living" messages from the heart of God, with the compassion of God and from the depths of God. He could only do this because God had "enraptured his heart," for "it is out of the heart that all things proceed":

Keep your heart with all diligence, for out of it spring the issues of life. (Proverbs 4:23)

Out of the abundance of the heart his mouth speaks. (Luke 6:45)

Deep calleth unto deep at the noise of thy waterspouts.
(Psalm 42:7 KJV)

Messages from God Must Proceed from the Heart

If the red-hot message of God is not in the heart, how can it proceed from the mouth? And how can the deep, burning, living messages of God be revealed to us unless God gets into the depths of our hearts?

Deep does not call to shallow, but to deep. As Wigglesworth said in another message entitled "Like Precious Faith,"

> A man is no better than what he is in his heart. Glossing over will not do; we must have the reality, we must have God, we must be able to go into God's presence and converse with Him.[16]

From my earliest days in Christ, I have longed for, prayed for, studied, and sought revival and harvest. Wigglesworth not only understood revival and harvest, but he also lived in the reality of revival and brought revival wherever he went. Revival flowed through him, from the depths of a heart where "deep had called to deep"—and multitudes of people were harvested for the kingdom of God.

> *Wigglesworth spoke burning, living messages out of the depths of his heart.*

In my pursuit of God's fullness and my endeavor to understand revival and the moving of the Spirit of God, I have studied both revivals and revivalists, and I have seen that God uses the heart of a man, a woman, or a group of people to be a catalyst through which revival is birthed.

The Difference between Revival and Harvest

Revival and harvest are two separate things, and we must see the distinction between them. The differences are very important. Revival is in the church, but harvest is in the world. Before we see the reaping of the great end-times harvest, we must see real, true revival in the church.

The people of this world cannot be taught the things of God until they are born again. It is a useless endeavor to try to teach them because these concepts and ways are totally alien to them. (See 1 Corinthians 2:14.) All they can see or understand is the face of Jesus revealed in a Christian man or woman, boy or girl. This will happen when we, the church, become "living letters" from Jesus to the world.

This essential communication of Christ to the world is spoken of in the book of Revelation as the *"spirit of prophecy"*:

> *For the testimony of Jesus is the spirit of prophecy.*
>
> (Revelation 19:10)

Harvest flows from Christians who reflect the nature, love, light, and power of Jesus Christ. Revival, on the other hand, brings Christians to the place of bearing this testimony. I pray that God may take you and me deeper and deeper into the revelation of revival, into the full reality of revival itself.

Revival Springs from the Incision of the Heart

As we study revival, we get a glimpse of where revival actually comes from. What we see is that revival springs from a heart that has had a deep, deep incision of the knife of God, which is the cross of Christ, to the point of the *"circumcision...of the heart"* (Romans 2:29).

This incision is like the work of the butcher when he takes his razor-sharp blade and skillfully separates the thick layer of fat from a side of beef. The knife of God, which, as I said, is the work of the cross of Christ, separates the carnal and useless being of flesh from the born-again one—the inner man who can produce nothing but life, for he is one with Christ. However, the incision must be deep. The deeper the incision, the more powerful the revival in the person's own life.

> *Deep calleth unto deep at the noise of thy waterspouts.*
>
> (Psalm 42:7 KJV)

The word *"waterspouts"* in this verse refers to large tubes of rotating cloud-filled wind, like funnels, that often hang from the clouds along the Mediterranean coast. They pour out vast torrents of rainwater on the earth.

In the context of revival, the *"waterspouts"* are the outpouring of God's blessing of revival on His people. After the personal revival of

> *As wildfire springs from tree to tree, revival fire springs from heart to heart.*

the incision of the heart, then the wonder of widespread revival begins. The Spirit of God leaps from heart to heart, and as *"deep calleth unto deep,"* the depth of that incision—and with it the revelation of the cross of Christ—calls out to another heart in spiritual transference of the very depth of that revelation. Then this other heart's owner, who is *"cut to the heart"* (Acts 2:37), also falls on his knees in horrifying recognition of what he himself really is and cries out to God for mercy. Through the marvelously mysterious work of the cross of Christ, he is also radically transformed to stand firm in the new man, who knows no bounds of love and adoration for Jesus Christ, the Bridegroom, his Lord.

In this way, *"deep calleth unto deep"* from one heart to another. As wildfire springs from tree to tree, revival fire springs from heart to heart, and the classic hallmarks of revival begin:

1. deep conviction
2. recognition of sin and failure
3. crying out to God for mercy
4. weeping as the cross cuts deeply

These are followed by:

5. great *"joy inexpressible and full of glory"* (1 Peter 1:8)
6. complete freedom
7. the height of loving and adoring worship of the Lord Jesus

All these go on and on to touch and transform everyone in the fire's path.

I believe that this is a glimpse of what we have longed for. It is, I am convinced, a divine glimpse into both what God has done before and what He is about to do again in these last days. It is a glimpse of what Wigglesworth was talking about in this message. The reality and extent of revival depend on the depth of the incision of the cross of Christ in the heart. As Wigglesworth knew and taught, "It is out of the heart that all things proceed."

In another message entitled "Flames of Fire," Wigglesworth also said,

> All His glory seems to fill the soul who is absolutely dead to self and alive to Him.

> There is so much talk about death, but I see that there is a death that is so deep in God, that out of that death God brings the splendor of His life and all His glory.[17]

Wigglesworth was talking about a deep incision of the work of the cross. He saw it, he embraced it, and it became both the determination and the secret of his life. It was not just talk with him, not just a concept, but a living reality to be lived and walked in.

We find, as we get a glimpse of revival and see both the reality of it and our need for it, that the fat and the flesh of self and pride are carved away. Our hearts cry out to God, "How can I serve You?" and the only answer that we hear is that we must fall to the ground and die (see John 12:24), and, laying hold of the cross, be fully crucified. (See Galatians 2:20.) This is so that we may become a pipeline of revival, bearing only "*the testimony of Jesus* [which] *is the spirit of prophecy*" (Revelation 19:10).

The reality and extent of revival depend on the depth of the incision of the cross of Christ in the heart.

Again and again in the lives of all the men and women who were used mightily by God, we see the reality that this deep work of the heart brings revival. We see it in the heart of Wigglesworth; in William Booth, founder of the Salvation Army; in Hudson Taylor, founder of the China Inland Mission; in John Wesley, evangelist, author, and founder of Methodism;

in George Whitefield, evangelist of the First Great Awakening; in John G. Lake, faith healer, missionary, and pastor; in evangelists Maria Woodworth-Etter and Charles Finney, and many, many others. It is the common thread of power that can be clearly seen in all revivalists. It is the work, once again, of the cross, the stone, and the fire.

> *The deep work of God in the heart comes only through incision or through breaking.*

For some of the revivalists, this work of the heart was brought about through the deep, deep incision of the cross of Christ, while in others, it was brought about through great brokenness wrought through the stone and the fire. That is, it came about either through the crisis of the heart that the deep revelation of the cross brings, or through a life-shattering crisis that the stone or the fire brings. We must realize that the deep work of God in the heart comes only through these two means: through incision or through breaking.

The Scriptures give us many pictures of this deep work of God. One of these, found in Hebrews, helps us greatly in understanding the way in which God works in our hearts.

> *For the word of God is living and powerful, and sharper than any two-edged sword, piercing even to the division of soul and spirit, and of joints and marrow, and is a discerner of the thoughts and intents of the heart.*   (Hebrews 4:12)

Just as the marrow is encased in the bone, the spirit of man is encased in the soul of man. As kernels of wheat are encased in the husk; as Gideon's army's lighted torches were encased in the earthen clay vessels (see Judges 7:12–25); as the spikenard ointment that anointed Jesus for His death was encased in an alabaster flask (see Mark 14:3–9), the *"inner man"* (Ephesians 3:16) is encased in the *"natural man"* (1 Corinthians 2:14).

From the analogy of the bone and the marrow, we understand that the bone must either be severed or broken in order to release the marrow. The bone may be polished smooth, but the marrow will never be released in that way. The bone may be "dressed up" so that it doesn't look like a bone anymore, but that won't release the marrow, either.

No, in the deep work of God in a person's life, the "bone" must be cut or broken—cut through a crisis of the heart by the deep work of the cross of Christ, or broken through a life-shattering crisis of trial and suffering. Only these processes will release the "marrow" of the anointing.

The Life-Shattering Crisis

As I mentioned previously, some Christians teach that this release of God's power and love comes only through trial and suffering, while other Christians discount this concept almost entirely, teaching that suffering is not of God. When we observe revival firsthand and study revival history, however, we find that God does use life-shattering crises to bring about the release of revival in a person's life. However, a life-shattering crisis is definitely not the only process that brings about revival; the work of the cross in the incision of the heart is also used by God in this way. It is important, therefore, that we understand both processes of God's work in the heart, as well as their validity and their application.

To a limited extent, I have seen firsthand the deep work of the life-shattering crisis and the release of revival in the life of a friend. This man was stopped short when he was diagnosed with a massive brain tumor and had to look death squarely in the face. Through this experience, he found the light of God exposing what was of his own making and what was of God's making in his life. He told me of this time, saying,

> It re-prioritized my life. The things that I had been driven to do before—to achieve success and build my ministry—seemed so unimportant in the face of cancer and death. I realized that I had neglected the most important things: my relationship with Jesus, nurturing and nourishing my wife, my children....I

had arrived, seemingly, at the American Dream—a nice house, two cars, a successful, growing ministry. But all these things became so unimportant.[18]

> *I could learn only from the deep communication of his heart to mine.*

My friend was supernaturally delivered of the cancer in a very dramatic and miraculous way while he was in the hospital, and there is a new sweetness in both his preaching and in the church that he pastors. An incision was made by the cross of Christ between flesh and spirit, old man and new man, in this man's life when he faced death. As a result, a definite element of revival came to his church, which became known for the sweetness of the presence of God in worship and the rich preaching of the Word.

The testimony of his miraculous healing has been written about in books and has been broadcast on television. It has inspired faith in many believers, has been of great encouragement to others who are sick, and has been *"a sign and a wonder"* (Deuteronomy 28:46; also see Acts 2) to nonbelievers. Yet the element of his experience that has intrigued me more than anything else is the opportunity that it afforded him to have his fleshly nature cut away and to draw so much closer to Christ.

I asked him once if he could share with me how I could learn the lessons he learned without facing such an extreme life-shattering crisis as terminal cancer, for many of us will not face such a crisis. Yet I discovered, as I listened to his answer, that I could not learn from his words but only from the deep communication of his heart to mine.

I have found the same thing to be true as I have gone through the process of learning and communicating the essence of Smith Wigglesworth's life and power. And it will be the same as we study any man or woman of God, for, though their messages remain with us in written word, we cannot learn from their words in the "natural order," but we must somehow hear their hearts, "for it is out of the heart that all things proceed."

It is for this reason that, when I discovered thirty-seven of Wigglesworth's sermons in a cupboard at the Home of Peace, an old missionary home in California, the Holy Spirit put it into my heart that I was not just to compile them and have them published, but to pray and seek God in order to see and understand the work that was done within his heart, for this is what would really be of benefit to others. As Wigglesworth would say, "A man is no better than what he is in his heart."

> **We need to learn to "hear" the hearts of revivalists, not just read their words.**

The fact that the work of the life-shattering crisis occurred in the hearts of many revivalists can be seen by the events of their lives and how they responded to them. Wigglesworth himself clearly faced death when he was stricken with appendicitis. Later, he lost his precious wife, and the following year he lost his son Ernest. He gave his life completely over to God in the midst of these extremely difficult circumstances, and he eventually ministered salvation and healing to thousands upon thousands around the world. His life was so affected by the cross, the stone, and the fire that his example has become a "living letter" of revival for the church.

We can also see the work of the life-shattering crisis in the life of Maria Woodworth-Etter, who lost five of her six children to the hand of death before they reached the age of ten. In her agonizing pain, she came to understand the reality of heaven by throwing herself upon God. She knew that she knew that she knew that her children were in a far better place; and the reality of this truth became so powerful in her life that, as she preached, "*deep call[ed] unto deep*" (Psalm 42:7 KJV), and people were stricken by this very reality. They would fall down in absolute conviction of sin, seemingly "slain" by the power of God, and they would find new life in Him. Miraculous healings also became the order of the day. Maria Woodworth-Etter became the catalyst of a revival through which thousands upon thousands were swept into the kingdom of God.

> *By embracing the fullness of the cross, many have become extraordinary in their fruitfulness for God.*

Aimee Semple McPherson lost her husband on the mission field of China. In the depths of her agonizing grief, she returned home to find the precious Cornerstone (see Matthew 21:42, 44); and, being broken by it, she also became the catalyst of a mighty revival that was the foundation of the Foursquare Gospel church, a movement that has affected the whole world. All of this happened because, when Aimee Semple McPherson allowed herself to be broken by the Cornerstone, "a grain of wheat fell to the ground and died, and because it died, it did not remain alone, but produced the fruit" of an international ministry. (See John 12:24.)

We could go on to look at many others who, through crisis and pain, have found the cross, the stone, and the fire, and have been extraordinary in their fruitfulness for God. However, the purpose of this book is not so much to examine the fullness of the release of revival power through pain and suffering, but rather to show how we can pursue and obtain this fullness by pressing into God—by embracing the revelation and impact of the cross of Christ through His Word, and by developing an intimacy with Him such as we have never before known. We can find it without necessarily having to face death or great suffering through a life-shattering crisis, for it is God's desire that we pursue Him and yield ourselves totally to Him out of our deep love and commitment to Him, regardless of the circumstances in our lives.

Although this pursuit of the cross is our focus, I fully realize that there are some who are reading this book who have faced, or who are now facing, a life-shattering crisis. If you are such a reader, my heartfelt prayer is that you may see the beauty of the reality of the deep work of God in the heart. I pray that, through your pain and hurt, you will embrace the cross of Christ and let it cut deeply to remove all that is of the "natural order" about you, so that the beauty of the One who lies within you may come forth, and so that others may see in you *"the testimony of Jesus* [which] *is the spirit of prophecy"* (Revelation 19:10).

The Crisis of the Heart

We have seen that there have been revivalists who experienced life-shattering crises that resulted in the breaking of the "bone" so that the "marrow" of the anointing could be released. There have also been a number of revivalists who experienced this deep work of the heart by pressing into God and experiencing the cutting of the bone in that way. These men and women had a deep "incision of the heart" without an extreme physical crisis or death in the family. Of these, there are a few that stand out in particular as living epistles (see 2 Corinthians 3:3), letters from God, showing us that this reality can be found without necessarily going through a physical or family crisis; it can be found by going through a spiritual crisis, or what we will call a "crisis of the heart."

> *God's desire for us is that we yield our hearts and lives completely to Him in love.*

One very powerful glimpse into the crisis of the heart can be seen in the conversion of Charles Finney. I would like us to briefly study his conversion as it is recorded in Winkie Pratney's book *Revival*:

Charles Finney:
The Cross and the Power

Charles was then studying to be a lawyer. While reading *Blackstone's Law Commentaries*, then the ultimate authority on the subject, he was struck by this Christian's constant reference to the Bible as the basis for all civil and moral law. He obtained a copy and began to study it seriously.

***

"The Spirit of God conducted me through the darkness and delivered me from the labyrinth and fog of a false philosophy, and set my feet upon the rock of truth—as I trust" (Finney, from the Preface, *Systematic Theology*).

His conversion read like something from the book of Acts. Under deep conviction from the Scripture, and dealt with by the Holy Spirit, he vowed one October Sunday evening in the fall of 1821, to "settle the question of my soul's salvation at once, that if it were possible I would make my peace with God" (Finney, *Autobiography*, p. 12).

For the next two days, his conviction increased, but he could not pray or weep; he felt if he could be alone and cry out loud to God something might happen. Tuesday evening, he became so nervous he felt if he did not cry out he would sink into hell, but he survived until morning. Setting out for work, he was suddenly confronted by an "inward voice" that riveted him to the spot in front of his office. "What are you waiting for? Did you not promise to give your heart to God? What are you trying to do—work out a righteousness of your own?"

The whole essence of conversion opened to him there in what he called "a marvelous manner"; the finished work of Christ, the need to give up his sins and submit to His righteousness. The voice continued, "Will you accept it, now, today?" Finney vowed, "Yes; I will accept it today or I will die in the attempt" (Finney, *Autobiography*, p. 15).

The Conviction of Sin

Sneaking away over the hill to a small forest where he liked to take walks, avoiding anyone who might ask him what he was doing, the young lawyer fought a battle with his pride. Several times he tried to pray, but rustling leaves stopped him cold; he thought someone was coming and would see him trying to talk to God. Finally near despair, thinking he had rashly vowed and that his hard-heartedness had grieved away the Holy Spirit, he had a sudden revelation of his pride: "An overwhelming sense of my wickedness in being ashamed to have a human being see me on my knees before God took such powerful possession of me that I cried at the top of my voice....I would not leave that place if all men on earth and all the devils in hell surrounded me....The sin appeared awful, infinite. It broke me down before the Lord" (Finney, *Autobiography*, p. 17).

Just then, a Scripture verse seemed to "drop into his mind with a flood of light": *"Then shall you go and pray to Me and I will hearken to you. Then shall you seek Me and find Me when you search for Me with all your heart"* (Jeremiah 29:12–13). It came to Finney with the flood of revelation, though he did not recall ever having read it. It shifted faith for him from the intellect to the choice; he knew that a God who could not lie had spoken to him and that his vow would be heard. Quietly, walking back toward the village, he was filled with such a sense of peace that it "seemed all nature listened." He realized it was noon; many hours had passed without any conscious sense of the passage of time.

A Divine Manifestation

Back at his office, his boss, Judge Wright, gone to lunch, Finney took down his bass viol and began to play and sing some hymns. "But as soon as I began to sing these sacred words, I began to weep. It seemed as if my heart were all liquid; my feelings were in such a state that I could not hear my own voice in singing without causing my sensibility to overflow....I tried to suppress my tears, but could not" (Finney, *Autobiography*, p. 20).

All that afternoon, filled with a profound sense of tenderness, sweetness, and peace, he helped Judge Wright relocate their office. The work finished, he bade his employer goodnight. "I had accompanied him to the door; and as I closed the door and turned around, my heart seemed to be liquid within me. All my feelings seemed to rise and flow out and the utterance of my heart was: 'I want to pour out my soul to God'" (Finney, *Autobiography*, p. 21). He rushed into a back room of the office to pray and then it happened:

"There was no fire, no light in the room; nevertheless it appeared to me as if it were perfectly light. As I went in and shut the door after me, it seemed as if I met the Lord Jesus Christ face to face. It did not occur to me then, nor did it for some time afterward, that it was a wholly mental state. On the contrary, it seemed to me that I saw Him as I would see any other man. He said nothing, but looked at me in such a manner as to break me down right at His feet....It seemed to me a reality that He stood before me and I fell down at His feet and poured out my soul to Him. I wept aloud like a child, and made such confessions as I could with a choked utterance. It seemed to me that I bathed His feet with my tears, and yet I had no distinct impression that I touched Him" (Finney, *Autobiography*, p. 21).

Baptized by the Spirit

For a long time, Finney continued in this state; eventually he broke off the interview and returned to the front office where the fire in the fireplace had nearly burned out. As he was about to take a seat by the fire, he received, in his own words, "a mighty baptism of the Holy Ghost. Without any expectation of it, without ever having the thought in my mind that there was any such thing for me, without any recollection that I had ever heard the thing mentioned by any person in the world, the Holy Spirit descended on me in a manner that seemed to go through me, body and soul. I could feel the impression, like a wave of electricity, going through and through me. Indeed, I could not express it any other way. It seemed like the very breath of God. I can recall distinctly that it seemed to fan me like immense wings.

"No words can express the wonderful love that was shed abroad in my heart. I wept aloud with joy and love; and I do not know but I should say, I literally bellowed out the unutterable gushings of my heart. These waves came over me and over me and over me, one after the other until I recollect I cried out, 'I shall die if these waves continue to pass over me.' I said, 'Lord I cannot bear it any more.' Yet I had no fear of death" (Finney, *Autobiography*, p. 22).

Later, a church choir member, knocking on his door, found him loudly weeping and asked if he was sick or in pain. Eventually able to speak, Finney said, "No, but so happy that I cannot live."

The Beginning of a Powerful Ministry

The following morning, with the sunlight, his baptism of power and love returned, and with it a call to the ministry. All that day each encounter with the lost led to powerful conviction and conversion. The first man he spoke to (his boss, the Judge) was struck with such conviction of sin that he could not look at him. He left the office under deep conviction, and a few days later was converted in the same woods where Finney himself was saved.

The second visitor, a client and a church deacon with a 10:00 A.M. case for the newly converted barrister to try for him, did not escape either. The young lawyer met him with the words, "I have a retainer from the Lord Jesus to plead His cause, and I cannot plead yours" (Finney, *Autobiography*, p. 26).

The next, a Universalist in a Christian shoemaker's shop, had his arguments demolished and headed over the fence to the woods and salvation.

From that day on, Finney realized it was good-bye to his legal profession. He launched out on a life of fire and power such as there have been few parallels in Christian history.[19]

Finney's story illustrates the stages we see in the lives of revivalists: conviction, separation, the "Jacobian struggle" (see Genesis 32:24–30), the cross, the anointing of the Holy Spirit, and the resulting ministry. *"So then death is working in us, but life in you"* (2 Corinthians 4:12). The glorious baptism in the Holy Spirit that Finney experienced and the incredible power that operated in his life to draw multitudes to Christ came from the depth of the experience he had with the cross. It was the depth of the incision of the knife of God, the cross of Christ, that cut so deeply and severed old from new, flesh from spirit, so radically that he was left weeping and could only say, "[I am] so happy that I cannot live."

> *Finney experienced a crisis of the heart that was life-altering.*

Finney experienced a crisis of the heart—a profound and very deep crisis of the heart through the cross of Christ. He found the depth of the cross without the life-shattering crisis in the external context of the rock and the fire that some other revivalists experienced because he found a life-shattering crisis internally, in the heart.

Remarkably, Finney experienced the depth of the incision, the crisis of the heart, over a period of a few days. With others, it took longer, for the heart surgery that was needed was different. However, I believe that the process is the same with all of us.

George Whitefield: To "Die or Conquer"

The second case study is that of the conversion of George Whitefield, whom I mentioned previously. His "incision of the heart" was a longer process than that of Finney's, but is very valuable to this study. Sadly, much of what scholars have written about Whitefield's tremendous impact for Christ speaks of great gifting and ability, of a "golden voice" and a "commanding eloquence."

The natural mind will always try to fathom how a man could be so enormously used by God and will come up with a reason that it was due to his gifts and abilities. I believe that Whitefield was not so much an enormously gifted man but an enormously crucified man. Again, these excerpts are taken from Winkie Pratney's book *Revival*:

> Sent off on his own at seventeen to Oxford for a chance to make it in life, he began to reevaluate his ways and think about his future.
>
> Convicted and lonely, under the dealings of the Holy Spirit, he became deadly serious about spiritual things; and in 1733 Charles Wesley invited him to join the Oxford "Holy Club." This gathering for spiritual discipline, Bible study, and prayer, though an object of Deist and Rationalist scoffing on campus, was not evangelical, famous, or even significant to the revival to come. It was only a legal attempt, by the Wesleys and others, to be better people. But it did not really meet any of their deep, inner needs. Here, young George read Henry Scougal's book *The Life of God in the Soul of a Man*, and it so directly contradicted all he believed that it alarmed him. In response to what he'd read, he said:

> "God showed me I must be born again or be damned! I learned a man may go to church, say his prayers, receive the sacraments and yet not be a Christian....Shall I burn this book? Shall I throw it down? Or shall I search it? I did search it; and holding the book in my hand thus addressed the God of heaven and earth: 'Lord, if I am not a Christian, or if I am not a real one, for Jesus Christ's sake show me what Christianity is that I may not be damned at last.'...From that moment...did I know that I must become a new creature" (Whitefield, *Journals*, p. 52).

Whitefield's ministry eventually impacted the world.

Fear Grips Whitefield

> Then followed not faith but a fearfully increased asceticism, with Whitefield wearing patched gown, dirty shoes, eating the

worst food, "whole days and weeks...spent lying prostrate on the ground...bidding Satan depart from me in the name of Jesus...begging for freedom from those proud hellish thoughts that used to crowd in upon and distract my soul" (Whitefield, *Journals*, p. 52).

For a year, the fearful pressure almost drove him mad, ruined his studies, and finally cost him his friendship in the Holy Club; he felt that perhaps his love for the other members was the final idolatry holding him back. Two years earlier, another club member, William Morgan, had lost his mind and his life; now Whitefield, grimly resolved to "die or conquer," seemed about to do the same. Finally, at the end of all human resources, God revealed Himself to the overjoyed young zealot. A gospel faith gave him the peace he had struggled so long to attain, and he wrote: "Oh what joy—joy unspeakable—joy full and big with glory was my soul filled when the weight of sin came off, and an abiding sense of the pardoning love of God and a full assurance of faith broke in on my...soul!"

Inspired Preaching

Sunday, June 27, in the church of St. Mary de Crypt, he preached his first sermon. His mother, relatives, Robert Raikes, the founder of the Sunday school, and some 300 other people crowded impatiently together to hear him. It was a startling introduction. Fifteen people were, said the presiding Bishop, "driven mad!" Whitefield was twenty-one years old. Thus began the "preaching that startled the nation."[20]

What transpired within this man's heart? The depth of the incision of the cross that he experienced through his personal Jacobian struggle against his own flesh and unbelief produced a remarkable ministry that touched the world. When Whitefield resolved to "die or conquer," he was saying, in effect, as Jacob had, *"I will not let You go unless You bless me!"* (Genesis 32:26). To know *"Christ and Him crucified"*

(1 Corinthians 2:2) became his life determination, and consequently "deep called to deep" in vast numbers of people, and he became a mighty *"waterspout"* (Psalm 42:7 KJV) for God.

KEY #3

THE DEATH OF THE NATURAL ORDER

No man is able to speak and bring forth the deep things of God out of his own mind....We cannot define, separate, or deeply investigate and unfold this holy plan of God unless we have the life of God, the thought of God, the Spirit of God, and the revelation of God.

The Deep Things of God

The "deep things of God"! Are they your desire? I hope so. For it is those who *"hunger and thirst"* who are filled (Matthew 5:6). Wigglesworth was a man who loved to "deeply investigate and unfold this holy plan of God." The deep things that he spoke of are the things beneath the surface, the treasures that need to be sought, the revelation of God's ways and of God Himself, things that Paul referred to as the *"mystery of Christ"*:

> By revelation He made known to me the mystery (as I have briefly written already, by which, when you read, you may understand my knowledge in the mystery of Christ). (Ephesians 3:3–4)

Paul went on to describe this mystery as *"the unsearchable riches of Christ"* (verse 8); he said that he was called *"to make all see what is the fellowship of the mystery,"* which had been *"hidden in God"* (verse 9), so that *"the manifold wisdom of God might be made known by the church to the principalities and powers in the heavenly places"* (verse 10). Then he spoke of God's *"eternal purpose which He accomplished in Christ Jesus our Lord"* (verse 11).

The deep things of God are treasures beneath the surface, the revelation of God Himself.

It is because God loves us that He reveals the wonders of the mystery of Christ and the deep things of His manifold wisdom. He takes all those who desire more of Him further and further into the revelation of *"the mystery of Christ"* as they seek Him and pray.

Wigglesworth had an awesome revelation of the mystery of Christ because he had paid the price of seeking and praying, of hungering and thirsting, to know more of God and the fullness of the deep things.

This is a book of *"solid food"* and not *"milk"* (1 Corinthians 3:2), and unfortunately it will be hard for some to understand. What we must realize is that we won't understand what Wigglesworth was getting at unless we really do seek God and pray to receive the revelation that he was teaching in these messages, which he had "defined, separated, and deeply investigated."

> *And I, brethren, could not speak to you as to spiritual people but as to carnal, as to babes in Christ. I fed you with milk and not with solid food; for until now you were not able to receive it, and even now you are still not able; for you are still carnal. For where there are envy, strife, and divisions among you, are you not carnal and behaving like mere men?*   (1 Corinthians 3:1–3)

It is a sad indictment, but honesty compels us to acknowledge that the Western church at the dawn of the twenty-first century is still very much afflicted with the carnality and the *"envy, strife, and divisions"* that Paul spoke of in this passage. If we are to understand or, in Wigglesworth's words, "define, separate, or deeply investigate and unfold this holy plan of God," we must separate ourselves from the carnality and strife of shallow Christianity and seek the Lord for "the life of God, the thought of God, the Spirit of God, and the revelation of God."

Praying the Prayer of Ephesians 3

The treasures of the mystery of Christ that are spoken of in the early verses of Ephesians 3 are in fact obtained by praying, on a continual basis, the prayer that follows in verses 14–19. If you will make this prayer your earnest, daily prayer, you will begin to see things, deep things in God, beyond what you've ever seen before:

> For this reason I bow my knees to You, Father, the Father of our Lord Jesus Christ, from whom the whole family in heaven and earth is named, that You would grant me, according to the riches of Your glory, to be strengthened with might through Your Spirit in my inner man, that Christ may dwell in my heart through faith; that I, being rooted and grounded in love, may be able to comprehend with all the saints what is the width and length and depth and height, and to know the love of Christ, which passes knowledge; that I may be filled with all the fullness of God. (Ephesians 3:14–19, adapted for personal use)

As I have prayed this prayer, one of the most powerful prayers that we can pray, God has led me into some very wonderful revelations. You can come *"to know the love of Christ which passes knowledge"* (verse 19). But, again, how can you *"know"* something that *"passes knowledge"*? As I briefly explained earlier, in this verse the Greek word for *"to know"* is *ginosko*, whereas the word "knowledge" in the phrase *"which passes knowledge"* is *gnosis*. *Ginosko* literally means "to be aware, feel, be resolved, be sure, understand." Essentially, it means to know experientially. However, *gnosis* means "knowledge, science." Basically, it means what can be stored in the human brain or in the data banks of the natural mind.

Ginosko is what God desires us to come into. It is the only way into the deep things of God that Wigglesworth spoke of. It is the *"hidden manna"* spoken of in Revelation 2:17. It is the food of the *"inner man"* (Ephesians 3:16), which we prayed,

> *God wants us to know Him experientially, not just know about Him factually.*

in the prayer from Ephesians 3, might be strengthened. I believe it is the missing ingredient in the many powerless saints of today's church.

> *To him who overcomes I will give some of the hidden manna to eat.*
> *And I will give him a white stone, and on the stone a new name*
> *written which no one knows except him who receives it.*
>
> (Revelation 2:17)

Seek the *ginosko* of the love of God as you read this book, as Wigglesworth did, *"that you may be filled with all the fullness of God"* (Ephesians 3:19, emphasis added).

KEY #4

THE VEIL MUST BE LIFTED

If we are going to get the best that God has for us, there must be a spiritual desire, an open ear, an understanding heart. The veil must be lifted. We must see the Lord glorified in the midst of us.

If the *"mystery of Christ"* (Ephesians 3:4) and of His cross is to be revealed to us in *ginosko* that transcends *gnosis*, then we must learn, as Wigglesworth spoke of, to live "beyond the veil"—beyond the veil of coldness, the veil of indifference, the veil of human reasoning, the veil of being self-satisfied, the veil of the natural order, for all these things are of the old man.

These veils separate us from *"the fellowship of the mystery"* (Ephesians 3:9), which God desires us to have. It is only the *"mystery of Christ"* and the fellowship we have with the mystery that will bring us into the power of God for revival.

How to Lift the Veil

But how is the veil to be lifted? Peter the apostle learned this lesson in a very abrupt but powerful way. As we examine the lesson that he learned, we too can learn the invaluable lesson of applying the cross to our understanding in the natural order. In this way, the veil will be taken away, so that we might, as Wigglesworth said, "get the best that God has for us."

> *From that time Jesus began to show to His disciples that He must go to Jerusalem, and suffer many things from the elders and chief priests and scribes, and be killed, and be raised the third day. Then Peter took Him aside and began to rebuke Him, saying, "Far be it from You, Lord; this shall not happen to You!" But He turned and said to Peter, "Get behind Me, Satan! You are an offense to Me, for you are not mindful of the things of God, but the things of men." Then Jesus said to His disciples, "If anyone desires to come after Me, let him deny himself, and take up his cross, and follow Me. For whoever desires to save his life will lose it, but whoever loses his life for My sake will find it."* (Matthew 16:21–25)

As we read this in the fullness of the context in which Jesus was speaking—for He always spoke in context—we see the power and reality of the cross as they pertain to the veil of the natural (carnal) mind. In this passage, Peter actually took Jesus aside and rebuked Him. Peter rebuked Him because of his "concern" for Him based on his own natural understanding of the situation. He did not have, as Wigglesworth referred to, "a spiritual desire, an open ear, an understanding heart." He did not have God's perspective, but the perspective of the natural man—his own perspective.

> *When we operate in the "old man," we allow Satan to have his way in us.*

Now, what is so striking about this is that Peter's man-centered perspective was so glaringly contrary, in fact, diametrically opposed, to God's perspective that Jesus turned and identified it as Satan literally having his way in Peter! Jesus said, *"You are an offense to Me!"* Who was an offense to Him? Satan, who was speaking through Peter's carnal mind. *"For you are not mindful of the things of God, but the things of men"* (Matthew 16:23).

Natural-mindedness is "stinkin' thinkin'" and must be brought to death.

We see clearly from this that Satan is *"mindful of the things of...men."* According to this, when we operate in the old man, the natural man, being mindful of the things of men, we are actually allowing Satan to have his way in us. In other words, natural-mindedness is "stinkin' thinkin'." That truth should give us pause to consider our actions before we operate in the natural man.

We can conclude, therefore, that the natural thinking of every man and woman is offensive to Jesus and must be brought to complete death. Thank God for His grace! It could just as easily have been you or I, instead of the apostle Peter, touting our opinions and understandings to the Lord, only to find the Lord pointing at us and saying, *"Get behind Me, Satan! You are an offense to Me, for you are not mindful of the things of God, but the things of men"* (Matthew 16:23).

This is why Jesus said to His disciples, immediately following His rebuke of Satan, who had been manifesting himself through Peter in this way, *"If anyone desires to come after Me, let him deny himself, and take up his cross, and follow Me"* (verse 24).

In the context of this verse, to "take up one's cross" means to deny the natural, or carnal, man. Yet from thousands upon thousands of pulpits around the world, it is preached and taught that our "cross" is the hardship we are facing, the sickness we are suffering, the financial setback we are experiencing, and so on. This is so far from the truth as to defy explanation! That is, any explanation except that the natural mind is very prevalent within so much of the church.

When Jesus told His disciples (and us) that they would have to deny themselves and take up their crosses and follow Him, He was clearly declaring something in the direct context of what had just happened. "Deny yourself!" That is, refuse to acknowledge self, the natural man. Take up your cross, which is the instrument of death (your personal appropriation of crucifixion). Be fully crucified, and then you will be fully following Him.

The desire to save any remnant of our old lives will end in compromise, and consequently keep us from God's fullness. Jesus said, *"Whoever loses his life for My sake will find it"* (Matthew 16:25). As Wigglesworth said in his sermon,

> There is not a natural thought that can be of any use here in this meeting. The natural life has to die completely, because there is no other plan for the baptized soul except to be *"dead indeed to sin"* (Romans 6:11).

The only way to go beyond the veil is through the cross. We must step out of the natural order into the spiritual realm; we must live as that new man whose name is not yet known (see Revelation 2:17), for he has "a spiritual desire, an open ear, an understanding heart." In this way, we will "get the best that God has for us."

The desire to save any remnant of our old lives will end in compromise and keep us from God's fullness.

We are just like the temple in Jerusalem at the time of the Crucifixion. As the thick veil of the temple was completely torn in two through the awesome power of the cross (see Luke 23:45), so must this same power tear apart the thick veil of the natural order within us, for we are the temple of God:

> *Do you not know that your body is the temple of the Holy Spirit who is in you?* (1 Corinthians 6:19)

The veil is the residue of the old man and all that the world formed him to be. Even though he is dead spiritually (see Colossians 3:3), unless the residue of the old man's influence—what the Bible calls *"the flesh"*—is dealt with through faith in God's Word, it can dominate our lives through the soul (the mind, feelings, and will). By recognizing the residue of "stinkin' thinkin'" in our souls, identifying it as the veil that holds us back from the fullness of God, we can know our enemy, and the veil can be lifted. Then we will "get the best that God has for us." As Wigglesworth said,

> We must clearly see that we are not going to be able to understand these mysteries that God is unfolding except along the lines of being filled with the Spirit.

> We must see that God has nothing for us along the old lines. The new plan, the new revelation, the new victories are before us. All carnal things, evil powers, and *"spiritual wickedness in high places"* (Ephesians 6:12 KJV) must be dethroned.

Walking in the Power of Revival

The infilling of the Holy Spirit, as Wigglesworth stated, is to bring us to the place where we understand the "mysteries that God is unfolding." The only way to reach this place is to move beyond the old lines, the old mind-set, and the old man.

God greatly desires to give us "the new plan, the new revelation, the new victories," and they "are before us," for they belong to the new man. But before we can fully enter them, "all carnal things, evil powers, and *'spiritual wickedness in high places'* (Ephesians 6:12 KJV) must be dethroned" in us. This will not be accomplished out there in the heavenlies somewhere; it will not be accomplished by shouting and binding some spirit in the atmosphere, but by personally, in our hearts and minds, dethroning "all carnal things, evil powers, and *'spiritual wickedness in high places'* (Ephesians 6:12 KJV)." Then, as Wigglesworth both taught and lived, we can walk in "the new plan, the new revelation, the new victories" in the power of revival!

KEY #5

I AM CRUCIFIED WITH CHRIST

What an ideal position, that now the sons of God are being manifested; now the glory is being seen; now the work is becoming an expressed purpose in life until the old life has ceased in them. How truly this position was shown forth in the life of Paul when he said,

I have been crucified with Christ; it is no longer I who live, but Christ lives in me; and the life which I now live in the flesh I live by faith in the Son of God, who loved me and gave Himself for me.

(Galatians 2:20)

Wigglesworth was one of the most powerful heralds of the baptism and infilling of the Holy Spirit to be used by God during the initial stages of the great outpouring of the twentieth century. His own experience of the baptism of the Holy Spirit was life-changing, and from the time of his experience, he went on to lead thousands upon thousands of Christians into the same experience.

> *The ideal place of complete "possession" by the Holy Spirit is awesome.*

He laid hold of the fullness of the baptism in the Holy Spirit perhaps more than any other person during the last century, and he found the place of total "possession" by the Spirit of God—an awesome place beyond his initial infilling where he became completely consumed and completely led by the Spirit of God. In this fullness, he found a direct link between the Acts 1:8 *"power [dunamis, Greek]"* of the infilling of the Holy Spirit and the 1 Corinthians 1:18 *"power [dunamis, Greek]"* of the cross, as he so clearly indicated in talking of the new day of the Holy Spirit:

What an ideal position, that now the sons of God are being manifested; now the glory is being seen; now the work is becoming an expressed purpose in life until the old life has ceased in them.

The Fullness of the Spirit Is to Bring the Fullness of the Cross

Wigglesworth stated clearly that the fullness of the Holy Spirit is to bring a ceasing of the "old life." It is to bring the fullness of the cross. As he said in another message, "Flames of Fire,"

> The baptism in the Holy Spirit has come for nothing less than to eat up the whole of my life. It set up Jesus as King, and nothing can stand in His holy presence when He is made King. [21]

What is prophecy? What is revival? It will be manifested where we are truly living witnesses of Jesus in power, glory, love, authority, wisdom, and life, because we are consumed by Him, possessed by His Spirit, and void of all that even hints of the old man. For "nothing can stand in His holy presence when He is made King." Essentially, the baptism in the Holy Spirit has been given to establish the death and life of the cross, the reality of,

> I [the old man] *am crucified with Christ: nevertheless I* [the new man] *live; yet not I, but Christ liveth in me: and the life which I* [the new man] *now live in the flesh I live by the faith of the Son of God* [His faith, not mine at all], *who loved me, and gave himself for me.* (Galatians 2:20 KJV)

Many people who teach about faith today use the words and example of Wigglesworth often in their preaching, and some truly understand him and have seen the elements of the death and life of the cross in the walk of faith that he had. But I hear many who totally miss this essential revelation that was the foundation, the very essence, of the power in his life. The secret to walking in Christ's power is to be fully crucified to this world.

> *The secret to walking in Christ's power is to be fully crucified to this world.*

If you desire to walk in revival faith, as Wigglesworth did, then you must *"live by the faith of the Son of God"* (Galatians 2:20 KJV), and only by His faith. There is no other way, for this is the priceless treasure that Wigglesworth found. In your own strength, your faith is no good, your life is no good, your plans are no good! It is only His faith, His life, His plans, that mean anything.

The efforts that you have made in working on yourself, improving yourself, sanctifying yourself, teaching yourself, rehabilitating yourself, and building up your faith must be replaced with *"His workmanship"* (Ephesians 2:10).

We Need the Baptism of Power

We see a church at the dawn of the twenty-first century twisted and stunted in comparison with God's church in the book of Acts, for so many Christians have built their lives on the sand of the rehabilitation of the natural man. (See Matthew 7:24–27.) When we do this, we build on our faith, our plans, and our lives, instead of building on the foundation of the cross. When we build on the foundation of the cross, our lives become completely replaced by the life of Christ; this is what the believers in Acts experienced.

> *We need glorious preaching and deep teaching on the cross.*

The cross must be set before us again and again in this day, for *"to us who are being saved it is the power [dunamis, Greek] of God"* (1 Corinthians 1:18). If the sons of God are to be fully manifest, if the army of the crucified is to rise to the *"mark…of the high calling"* (Philippians 3:14 KJV) of following the King of Kings and Lord of Lords in the great and final battle, if the bride of Christ is to fully shed the old garment to shine forth in the new, then we need the baptism of power that comes through the cross.

We need preaching, glorious preaching, on the cross. We need teaching, deep teaching, on the cross.

We Need to Emphasize Christ Crucified

Not with wisdom of words, lest the **cross of Christ** *should be made of no effect.*　　　　　(1 Corinthians 1:17, emphasis added)

What does the word *lest* in this verse indicate? Using the wisdom of human words is the equivalent of making the cross of Christ of no effect! We need to determine, as Paul did, *"not to know anything…except Jesus Christ and Him crucified"* (1 Corinthians 2:2). When Paul determined this, he had just come from Athens in Greece. He had been in his element at the Areopagus. He had been surrounded by the intellectuals of the known world of that time, who *"spent their time in nothing else but either to tell or to hear some new thing"* (Acts 17:21). Paul had spoken powerfully to them of the nearness of God. He had woven a rich tapestry of important subjects, including idolatry, repentance, judgment, and Jesus' resurrection. After all, he was one of their peers, and Paul was as skillful an orator as the best of them.

> *We need to guard against stepping back into our natural strengths and old gifts.*

Up to this time, his ministry had been one of miracles, citywide harvests of souls, riots, divine intervention through an earthquake, visions, and a phenomenal spreading of God's kingdom to thousands of Gentiles. It had been a ministry of revival and harvest. But on this important occasion, in the apparent absence of one particular message, the simplicity and power of the message of the cross—that Christ died for the sins of mankind on the cross of Calvary to pay the price for our redemption, becoming sin for us so that we might be made the righteousness of God in Him and have eternal life (see 2 Corinthians 5:21)—in the neglect of this message that is *"the power of God"* (Romans 1:16), we read of a different result:

And when they heard of the resurrection of the dead, some mocked, while others said, "We will hear you again on this matter." So Paul departed from among them. However, some men joined him and believed.

(Acts 17:32–34)

"*However, some men joined him and believed.*" No miracles, no riots, no clamoring, no great harvest.

The book of Acts tells us that after his experience at the Areopagus, Paul departed immediately from Athens for some reason and sailed to Corinth. (See Acts 18:1.) When we find him next, he is a very different Paul. He is "*in weakness, in fear, and in much trembling*" (1 Corinthians 2:3). To the church at Corinth, Paul afterwards wrote about this time, saying,

> *And I, brethren, when I came to you, did not come with excellence of speech or of wisdom declaring to you the testimony of God. For I determined not to know anything among you except Jesus Christ and Him crucified. I was with you in weakness, in fear, and in much trembling. And my speech and my preaching were not with persuasive words of human wisdom, but in demonstration of the Spirit and of power, that your faith should not be in the wisdom of men but in the power of God.* (1 Corinthians 2:1–5)

Why did Paul leave immediately following the incident in Athens? Why was he "*in weakness, in fear, and in much trembling*" when he got to his next destination? From studying these Scriptures in light of the power of the message of the cross, I believe that at the Areopagus, Paul stepped back into his natural strengths and old gifts. He returned to the intellectual discourse and eloquence that the natural man considers so profound, and it scared him. It scared him desperately—so much so that it sent him reeling to Corinth "*in weakness, in fear, and in much trembling.*"

He had seen the result of the natural man: "*However, some men joined him and believed*" (Acts 17:34). But he had also felt the frightening absence of the "*demonstration of the Spirit and of power*" (1 Corinthians 2:4), and he saw with crystal

> *Self-improvement techniques may satisfy the natural man, but will leave the real you feeling empty.*

clarity that if his old self were allowed to come forth again, then any real ministry of the caliber that he had known was over. Therefore, clinging to the cross unto the crucifixion of the natural man, he declared with all his heart, *"I determined not to know anything among you except Jesus Christ and Him crucified"* (1 Corinthians 2:2).

Many wonder why we see a church today in which the reality of *"However, some men joined him and believed"* prevails, while the *"demonstration of the Spirit and of power,"* in the context of the book of Acts, continues to be an illusive dream. I believe it is because of the missing determination to know nothing else *"except Jesus Christ and Him crucified."* We need the cross. The body of Christ worldwide must come to the place, as Paul did, where we determine to lay aside all else, before we will see the great and glorious return of our King.

So much of the teaching we hear in this day and age is similar in that it appeals to the natural man. It teaches him much about how to improve himself, how to make his family life better, and how to increase his finances. He so easily falls for this wonderful "wisdom," taught with such eloquence, and he applies it to his life and improves himself, only to find that this is not the real call of God on his life and that it ends in mediocrity. The real call of God on my life and yours is that the natural man be crucified, annihilated, mortified. It must be thoroughly put to death.

> *Determine to lay aside everything else but the cross.*

Many people have left the cross, "advanced" to self-improvement, and have stopped the process of being fully saved, which is the replacement of self with a totally new man in the image of God.

> *For the message of the cross is foolishness to those who are perishing, but to us who are **being saved** it is the power of God.*
> (1 Corinthians 1:18, emphasis added)

When we leave this determination of Paul's *"not to know anything among you except Jesus Christ and Him crucified"* (1 Corinthians 2:2), we begin to perish again for, in our natural man, we are of the company of *"those who are perishing."* In the light of the *"excellence of speech or of wisdom"* (1 Corinthians 2:1) and the *"persuasive words of human wisdom"* (verse 4) that the natural man loves, and which do undoubtedly have some effect on changing and rehabilitating him for the better, the simplicity of the cross falls into unimportance, because it is truly *"foolishness"* to the natural mind. In fact, this book will undoubtedly be absolute foolishness to some.

> *But even if our gospel is veiled, it is veiled to those who are perishing.* (2 Corinthians 4:3)

The beauty and reality of the fullness of the gospel is veiled to the natural mind, for the natural mind is of *"those who are perishing."*

> *Therefore we do not lose heart. Even though our outward man is perishing, yet the inward man is **being** renewed day by day.* (2 Corinthians 4:16, emphasis added)

The outward man veils or conceals the inward man, just as the natural mind veils or obscures the *"mind of Christ"* (1 Corinthians 2:16) within. The *gnosis* alone will never lead us to the mind of Christ—we must have the *ginosko*. We must pass beyond mere knowledge and concepts, and we must come to know it in the depths of our hearts, in the inner man. This is part of the essence of revival!

KEY #6

THE HEIGHT OF EXALTATION

Oh, beloved, may our God, the Holy Spirit, have His way today in thus unfolding to us the grandeurs of Christ's glory.

> *And we have such trust through Christ toward God. Not that we are sufficient of ourselves to think of anything as being from ourselves, but our sufficiency is from God.* (2 Corinthians 3:4–5)

Ah, it is lovely! Those verses are all too deep to pass over. That is the height of exaltation, which is so different from human exaltation. We need to get to a place where we are beyond trusting in ourselves.

Beloved, there is so much failure in self-assurances. We must never rest upon anything in the human. Our trust is in God, and God brings us into victory. When we have no confidence in ourselves, then our whole trust rests upon the authority of the mighty God.

Repeatedly, Wigglesworth pointed to the message of the cross. "The height of exaltation, which is so different from human exaltation" is that message. The height of exaltation is the point at which we have gone so far beyond trusting in ourselves, our abilities, our intellects, and our eloquence that the *"demonstration of the Spirit and of power"* (1 Corinthians 2:4) may be fully manifested in us.

"There is so much failure in self-assurances." We must see that it is not the "army of the gifted" but the "army of the crucified" that will reap the great end-times harvest! Yet, sadly, it is the army of the gifted that we see running the church in so many instances, and doing the work of the "ministry," and we wonder why we do not have revival.

Most gladly therefore will I rather glory in my infirmities, that the power of Christ may rest upon me.   (2 Corinthians 12:9 KJV)

"Glory in my infirmities"? Oh, how Paul knew the cross. He knew it so deeply and so wonderfully. He was saying here, "I will be proud only of how weak and incapable I, Paul, am, for I desire only *'the power of Christ'* and none of the 'power of Paul.'" As he wrote in Philippians 3, "'All things that were gain to me, I counted as loss' (see verse 7 KJV)—all my abilities, my learning, my gifts, everything. I will not, I cannot, be proud of them. I consider them absolute *'dung'* (verse 8 KJV), or *'rubbish'* (verse 8), for this is the only way that I may *'gain Christ'* (verse 8). And I must gain Christ, for I desire more than any other thing *'the excellence of the knowledge of Christ'* (verse 8)."

When we have a clear understanding of this prophetic walk in the power of Christ, when it becomes our greatest desire and we come to know that we cannot have it if we receive the *"honor of man"* (see John 5:41–44), our hearts cry out to others, "Please do not honor me, for in myself I am of no value, but I pray that you may see *'Christ in* [me], *the hope of glory'* (Colossians 1:27)." This was the cry of Wigglesworth's heart.

> *The "army of the crucified," not the "army of the gifted," will reap the harvest.*

Beloved, there is so much failure in self-assurances. We must never rest upon anything in the human. Our trust is in God, and God brings us into victory. When we have no confidence in ourselves, then our whole trust rests upon the authority of the mighty God.

The secret to life is death. When we die to ourselves, we gain the height of exaltation—the life of Christ within us. And when we physically die and go to be with Christ forever, we will gain Him in the ultimate sense. As Paul said, *"For to me, to live is Christ, and to die is gain"* (Philippians 1:21).

Jesus said, *"He who finds his life will lose it"* (Matthew 10:39). Truly, "there is so much failure in self-assurances" and in our own lives. However, the person who finds His life, the Christ-life, will find the only life worth living. He will find "the height of exaltation, which is so different from human exaltation." And *"he who loses his life,"* (verse 39), the self-life, will find abundant life.

The height of exaltation is *"the honour that cometh from God only"* (John 5:44 KJV). This far exceeds human exaltation, which is *"honor from men"* (John 5:41; see verse 44)—both self-honor and honor that comes from others. I am more and more coming to the realization of what Wigglesworth was saying here—the realization that I cannot have any trust in myself, for the natural man is thoroughly untrustworthy. But when I have absolutely no confidence in myself, I find that my "whole trust rests upon the authority of the mighty God."

The reality of this truth is so beautiful! It is the "height of exaltation"! Wigglesworth fully lost his self-life and found the fullness of Another's life. That was the secret of his power, and if you observe closely, you will see it in all of his messages. He became a herald of both Pentecost and the army of the crucified.

This book is dedicated to the army of the crucified, for they are the only army that will reap the great end-times harvest. They are those who will take hold of the cross and embrace the death to self that it brings, so that they may be pure vessels for the anointing and power of the Holy Spirit.

The Jacobian Struggle

These words were written by the late Keith Green:

> My flesh is tired of seeking God,
> But on my knees I'll stay.
> I want to be a pleasing child
> Until that final day.[22]

***

> My eyes are dry, my prayers are cold;
> My heart is hard, my faith is old.
> But I know how I ought to be,
> Alive to You and dead to me.
>
> But what can be done with an old heart like mine
> But to soften it up with oil and wine?
> The oil is You, Your Spirit above.
> Please wash me anew in the wine of Your love.[23]

The songs of Keith Green stirred the church around the world and were instrumental in bringing revival to thousands upon thousands of young hearts. I truly believe he was a revivalist. His music opened up the Christian music industry in a new way and established a new day for it.

However, the phenomenal success of his music was not because of its brilliance. His musical gifts were very evident, yet we have seen even more "brilliant" and "gifted" people since him whose music has had nowhere near the impact that Keith Green's music had. It poured forth from his heart rather than from his giftedness. It poured forth from a heart that had had a deep incision of the cross, a heart of brokenness, a heart that maintained the Jacobian struggle, that said, as Jacob did, "*I will not let You go unless You bless me!*" (Genesis 32:26). And because of the incision of the cross and his maintaining the determination to be "alive to You and dead to me," revival flowed through his music to a whole generation.

Even though his music established a new day, a new open door, in Christian music, we have seen the Christian music industry filled with primarily the army of the gifted and not the army of the crucified, to which Keith belonged. Keith was by no means fully crucified, for he was infamous for the times when he moved out of the new man and back into the old man. (I say this in view of Keith's own acknowledgment in his tract entitled, "For Prophets Only."[24]) Yet he lived in the struggle to be dead to self—the Jacobian struggle—and because of this, his songs came to us with the true blessing of God in brokenness, and we heard not the old man, but the new man.

Tragically, we have seen artists since his time reach fame and success while in adultery, marital breakdown, drugs, and personal defeat. Please understand me. I am not throwing stones at these people. I love them and genuinely feel the compassion of Christ for them in their hurt and defeat, for they merely became the products of a church that honored their great gifts alone. They became the products of a wrong perspective based on the "natural" way of thinking, the carnal mind—and the carnal mind brings forth only death. (See Romans 8:6.)

We have our eyes on gifts, to the great demise of revival, which springs from a

Revival is available to us right now through embracing the cross.

heart that has had a true incision of the cross of Christ. In our pursuit of the gifted, we have made "kings" for ourselves (see 1 Samuel 8:4–7), and we have been left wondering where the power of Christ for revival has gone, hoping that maybe someday, somehow, God will sovereignly pour down revival from heaven. Yet it has been available to us all the time through embracing the cross!

In the book of Genesis, we see in Jacob's metamorphosis from *Jacob*, the cheat and deceiver, whose name means "supplanter," to *Israel*, which means "prince of God," a foreshadowing of the process of the cross. Jacob lived for many years by his own wits, his own gifts, and his own abilities, and he did not find God's plan for his life; he remained merely "Jacob." But he came to a point in his life when he faced something that he, in himself, could not handle. He experienced what I have come to call a "life-shattering crisis," which brought him to a "crisis of the heart," and he separated himself from everyone and everything to meet with the Lord alone. There, Jacob wrestled with the Lord. He had lived for too long under a cheater's blessing, stolen through his own cunning from his brother Esau. He had to be brought to the realization that it wasn't the real thing. He needed the real blessing of God, not one of his own making.

And so Jacob wrestled with the Lord. With a newfound tenacity, he said, "I must have the blessing. I cannot go on without it. I will not let You go. I cannot. For without the real blessing, life is pointless." (See Genesis 32:26.) It was at this juncture that the real blessing became his absolute determination, his "magnificent passion." Jacob said, "*I will not let You go unless You bless me!*" (verse 26).

Then the blessing came. But it came in an unexpected way. It came when the Lord reached down and, with His divine touch, did not supercharge him, delight him, or bless him in any natural way, but rather crippled and broke him. He broke him of his own ways and abilities, his own gifts and achievements, and from that day, Jacob walked with a limp, a limp that marked the day when he had "met face-to-face with the Lord and lived." (See verse 30.) Yet "Jacob" didn't live, for on that day "Jacob" died and "Israel" was born. (See verse 28.)

Looking for the Great Rising

I have come to the place where it seems I'm not impressed with gifts or abilities anymore; I find myself looking for a man with a limp. A man or woman *"poor in spirit"* (Matthew 5:3). Someone who has met "face-to-face with God," who has wrestled with Him until he has been broken and the cross has cut deeply. This is a person who will bring revival. We must look for a man or woman who bears the *"marks of the Lord Jesus"* (Galatians 6:17)—the marks that he or she has been crucified and then resurrected. We must look for a man or woman out of whose heart flows the beauty of the cross, who lives in the magnificent passion of being dead to self and fully alive to God. And even beyond this, we must look for the great rising of an army of such men and women, beautiful and powerful, adorned and clothed solely with Christ. They are the bride of Christ. They are the army of the crucified.

Wigglesworth, Whitefield, Finney, Kathryn Kuhlman, and all the other revivalists were people with a limp. Out of their hearts flowed the reality of brokenness and a crucified life—the essence of revival.

What an ideal position, that now the sons of God are being manifested; now the glory is being seen; now the work is becoming an expressed purpose in life until the old life has ceased in them.

Therefore He is also able to save to the uttermost those who come to God through Him, since He always lives to make intercession for them. —Hebrews 7:25

PART 3:

UTTERMOST SALVATION

UTTERMOST SALVATION

To begin this section, I'd like you to read another remarkable account from the life of Smith Wigglesworth.

"A Little Touch of Heaven"

"I will stay tonight, no matter what it takes."

Pastor Harry Roberts affirmed in his heart that he would do whatever it took to stay in the prayer meeting that was held in the back room prior to the revival meeting. The revival meetings had been very powerful. So many sick had been healed, so many new people had been born again, and so many Christians had been set on fire by the baptism in the Holy Spirit. The evangelist that God was using so mightily to bring the whole district alive was the Englishman Smith Wigglesworth. He had been staying in Pastor Roberts' home, and the presence and peace of God had filled the home in a whole new way during his stay. Roberts had had some wonderful fellowship with Wigglesworth in his home as they had shared the things of God together. He had also had the opportunity to get a glimpse of the depth of God and the depth of brokenness in this most unusual man through whom the power of God moved so incredibly— such as the time when Wigglesworth had shared, with tears in his eyes, how he had lost the most precious thing in all the world to him, his wife.

However, when it came to the prayer meeting prior to the revival meeting, it was different. Night after night, pastors, elders, young evangelists, and intercessors had crowded into the back room to pray, and pray they did, until Wigglesworth began to pray. When this uneducated, broken man of God began to pray, he prayed right into heaven, and heaven seemed literally to fill the room. The presence of God became so intense that, one by one, each of them was forced to leave—convicted, overpowered, and physically unable to stay. But tonight, vowed Pastor Roberts, would be different. No matter what it took, he was going to stay.

> *When Wigglesworth prayed, heaven seemed to fill the room.*

The prayer meeting had already begun when the commanding figure of Smith Wigglesworth came in, immaculately dressed in a dark suit, bringing with him an immediate heightening of God's presence. In due time, he began to pray, and once again it seemed as if heaven had come and filled the room. One by one, they had to leave. Pastor Roberts' heart was racing. "I will stay. I must stay. Lord, please let me stay." Soon everyone else had left, and he was the last one remaining with Wigglesworth. As Wigglesworth prayed right into heaven, Roberts felt himself being physically forced out of the room. He fell to the floor, unable to stand. He must stay. In front of him was a large wooden chair. He latched onto it, hoping that it would be an anchor, desperate to stay, whatever it took.

Wigglesworth prayed on, caught up in God, seemingly oblivious of both chair and man as they were together forced from the room by the presence of God, before whom no flesh can stand.[1]

The Nature of Anointing

This remarkable true story of those who experienced praying with Wigglesworth illustrates a real phenomenon. It reveals the degree to which Wigglesworth had experienced the death of the cross. It shows what happens when a man allows the cross of Christ to crucify his flesh

(Galatians 5:24) so that he becomes a pure channel for the anointing and presence of God.

The Bible tells us that *"no flesh should glory* [or boast] *in His presence"* (1 Corinthians 1:29,). The Greek word for *"flesh"* in this verse is *sarx*, which includes the meaning of "human nature (with its frailties [physical or moral] and passions)." I believe that this testimony about Wigglesworth indicates to us that the measure to which we both pray and operate in the anointing is proportionate to the measure to which the flesh has been removed from our lives.

Wigglesworth, through prayer, actually brought the presence of God, the anointing and the reality of God, into our earthly human reality in both that prayer room and in his meetings, to the extent that it actually superseded the reality that we know with our senses! This anointing brought a force to bear on everything in its path that removed whatever was not in total unity with God. Just as whatever was of the flesh could not remain in that prayer room, so also, under this same anointing, sin had to go, sickness had to go, satanic oppression had to go from the people who attended his meetings.

This anointing was the essence of the signs, wonders, miracles, and revivals that occurred in the ministries of all the great revivalists of history. Their dying to the flesh made them channels that brought the life of Christ to the multitudes who came to sit under their ministries. Hallelujah!

Now let us turn to another sermon of Smith Wigglesworth's, entitled "Uttermost Salvation," to learn more keys to revival from his life and teachings.

UTTERMOST SALVATION

A Message by Smith Wigglesworth

Blessed are the poor in spirit, for theirs is the kingdom of heaven. Blessed are those who mourn, for they shall be comforted. Blessed

are the meek, for they shall inherit the earth. Blessed are those who
hunger and thirst for righteousness, for they shall be filled.

(Matthew 5:3–6)

Many people say that the fifth chapter of Matthew is for the millennial age and that people cannot live it now. Consequently, they avoid this chapter without carefully investigating it. But for the spiritually mature, there is a little heaven on earth in the truth of this passage. Mature Christians can reach a place where they have no fellowship with darkness and where the world does not know them.

After I was baptized in the Holy Spirit, I saw distinctly that God had allowed me to eat of that Tree of Life of which Adam and Eve were not able to eat. I saw that when the Holy Spirit came in, He wonderfully revealed Christ to me so that I was nourished by His presence, strengthened, and filled with great joy. Praise His name! I know that the baptism of the Holy Spirit brings us into possession of all the fullness of God. People often sing, "Oh, that will be glory for me. When by His grace, I shall look on His face," but I saw that God had changed that song for me so that I can sing:

> Oh, now it is glory for me,
> Now it is glory for me,
> For as by His grace,
> I look on His face,
> Now it is glory for me.

Let me now come to this wonderful chapter God has given. I will begin with the third verse, *"Blessed are the poor in spirit, for theirs is the kingdom of heaven"* (Matthew 5:3). The people who have grasped this idea and have identified themselves with the Lord Jesus Christ have come to a place where they now see that all things are possible with God. We have come to a place of an unlimited supply in God, and in our poverty of spirit, we are entitled to all that God has, *"for theirs is the kingdom of heaven."* In spite of my meekness, humility, and helplessness, all that God has is mine.

When Jesus came to Sychar, a city of Samaria, *"being wearied from His journey"* (John 4:6), He sat down by a well. His disciples were not with Him because they had gone to buy food in a nearby city (John 4:8). When they returned, they saw Him at peace. He was not looking for food but was quite relaxed. When Jesus was not interested in eating the food they had bought, *"the disciples said to one another, 'Has anyone brought Him anything to eat?'"* (verse 33). This shows us the possibility for man to live in God, to be absorbed in God, with no consciousness of the world under any circumstances, except as we bring help to it. And He said to them, *"Behold, I say to you, lift up your eyes and look at the fields, for they are already white for harvest!"* (verse 35). That is His food, the spiritual life in God, which is joy in the Holy Spirit.

He comes to enrapture our souls, to break every bond of mere human affection and replace in us the divine instead of the earthly, the pure instead of the unholy, the eyes of faith that see God instead of human feelings. The divine Son of God is to be in us, mightily moving through us, as we cease to be. Nothing helps us in the human place but this poverty of spirit, spoken of in this Beatitude.

We must live in such a pure atmosphere that God will shine in and through our souls. Oh, this uttermost salvation (Hebrews 7:25)! I am satisfied that as we get to know the Son of God, we will never be weak anymore. The tide will turn. Let us look at the next verse in Matthew 5: *"Blessed are those who mourn, for they shall be comforted"* (verse 4).

Did Jesus mean mourning over death? No, He meant mourning over our sons and daughters who have not yet touched heaven, who know nothing about the things of the Spirit of Life. When God places within us a mourning cry to move the powers of God, then He will send a revival in every home.

It is impossible to get this spiritual mourning over lost souls without having the very next thing that God says, "[You] *shall be comforted.*" As though God could give you a spirit of mourning over a needy soul, and then not give you victory! Beloved, it is the mighty power of God in us. And when the Spirit brings us to this mourning attitude over lost souls and over all the failures that we see in professing Christians, until we can go into the presence of God with that mourning spirit, nothing will happen. But when that happens, rejoice; God will bring you through.

God wants us to rejoice today. He has brought us into this blessed place so that we may mourn and then rejoice. Let us go on with the chapter because much depends on the next verse: *"Blessed are the meek, for they shall inherit the earth"* (Matthew 5:5).

You say, "Don't talk to me about being meek; I will never be able to be like that." Take the case of Moses. He surely was not meek when he killed the Egyptian. But when God got Moses into His hand in the land of Midian, He molded him so that he became the meekest man in all the earth. I do not care what your temper is like. If you get only a little touch of heaven, God can mold you so that you can be the meekest person on the earth.

I used to have such a bad temper that it made me tremble all over. It would make me furious with its evil power. I saw that this temper had to be destroyed; it could not be patched up. One day the power of God fell upon me. I came to the meeting and fell down before the Lord. The people began asking, "What sin has Wigglesworth been committing?" This went on for two weeks. Every time I came to the altar, God used to sweep through me with such a manifestation of my helplessness that I would go down before God and weep right through. Then the preacher or the leader would be broken up and come beside me. God started a revival that way. God had broken me up, and revival began through His revival in me. Oh, it was lovely! At last my wife said, "Since my husband had that touch, I have never been able to cook anything that he was not pleased with. It is never too cold and never too hot."

Only God can make people right. Only melted gold is minted. Only moistened clay accepts the mold. Only softened wax receives the seal. Only broken, contrite hearts receive the mark as the Potter turns us on His wheel. Oh, Lord, give us that blessed state where we are perfectly and wholly made meek.

What a wonderful chapter this is. The Beatitudes of the Spirit are truly lovely. *"Blessed are those who hunger and thirst for righteousness, for they shall be filled"* (Matthew 5:6). Oh, yes, praise the Lord! We must emphasize that God will not fail to fill us. No man can "hunger and thirst after righteousness" unless God has put the desire in him. And I want you to notice that this righteousness is the righteousness of Jesus.

In 1 John 5:4–5, we find these verses: *"This is the victory that has overcome the world; our faith. Who is he who overcomes the world, but he who believes that Jesus is the Son of God?"* Righteousness is more than paying our way. We hear someone say, "Oh, I never do anything wrong to anybody. I always pay my way." This is simply life in the flesh, but there is a higher *"law of the Spirit of life in Christ Jesus"* (Romans 8:2). I must see that Jesus is my perfect righteousness. He came by the power of God:

> *For what the law could not do in that it was weak through the flesh, God did by sending His own Son in the likeness of sinful flesh, on account of sin: He condemned sin in the flesh.* (Romans 8:3)

We must see that if we get this righteousness of God, sin is destroyed. There are beautiful words in the ninth verse of the first chapter of Hebrews: *"You have loved righteousness and hated lawlessness; therefore God, Your God, has anointed You with the oil of gladness more than Your companions."*

But the height of divine touches of heaven never leaves you stationary but rather increases your thirst and appetite for greater things. Something within makes you press on until you are empty of everything else so that you may be filled with what God is pressing in. This righteousness is a walk with God. It is a divine inheritance. It is seeing the face of Jesus until you cannot be satisfied without drinking of His Spirit and being overflowed continually with His blessings. I cannot be satisfied without Christ's righteousness. He gives us thirst for the immensity of God's power. It is a divine problem that is solved in only one way: having Him. And having Him, we have all things.

I pray that God will bring you to a death of self and a life of righteousness, which will please God in the Spirit. Thus we understand in some measure what God has for us in the next verse of Matthew 5: *"Blessed are the merciful, for they shall obtain mercy"* (verse 7).

I believe this is truly a spiritual condition, which is higher than the natural law. Sometimes when we talk about mercy, we think of being kind, amiable, or philanthropic toward others. We think those are respected positions. So they are, but the world has that. Beloved, we should have all that, but we should have much more.

We will never understand the meaning of the mercy of Jesus until He fills us with Himself. My blessed Lord! Can there ever be one like Him? Can you think of such rarity, such beauty, such self-sacrifice? *"Blessed are the merciful."* We must have heaven's riches to give to souls in poverty. You cannot be filled with the Lord and not be merciful. You cannot have the baptism with power without this supernatural mercy, this divine touch of heaven that stops satanic forces, frees the oppressed, and strengthens the helpless. That is the spirit that God wants to give us. Oh, for heaven to bend down upon us with this deep inward cry for a touch of Him, His majesty, His glory, His might, His power!

It is a very remarkable thing that the merciful always obtain mercy. Look at the measure of this spiritual life: first full, then pressed down, then shaken together, and then running over (Luke 6:38). This divine touch of heaven is lovely. It is the most charming thing on earth, sweeter than all. I am just running over with new wine this morning. God wants you to have this new wine. It thrills the human heart. How it mightily sweeps you right into heaven!

I ask you all, needy souls, whatever you want, to *"come boldly to the throne of grace"* (Hebrews 4:16). Come, and the Lord bless you.

KEY #1

HIDDEN MANNA

When Jesus came to Sychar, a city of Samaria, *"being wearied from His journey"* (John 4:6), He sat down by a well. His disciples were not with Him because they had gone to buy food in a nearby city (verse 8). When they returned, they saw Him at peace. He was not looking for food but was quite relaxed. When Jesus was not interested in eating the food they had bought, *"the* disciples said to one another, 'Has anyone brought Him anything to eat?'" (John 4:33). This shows us the possibility for man to live in God, to be absorbed in God, with no consciousness of the world under any circumstances, except as we bring help to it. And He said to them, "*Behold, I say to you, lift up your eyes and look at the fields, for they are already white for harvest!*" (verse 35). That is His food, the spiritual life in God, which is joy in the Holy Spirit.

The nature of Christ within, the very proof of "*Christ in you, the hope of glory*" (Colossians 1:27), the very sustenance of a man or woman living in God, absorbed in Him, is harvest! It is bringing men and women, boys and girls, to Christ. The "*food*" (John 4:32, 34) that refreshed Jesus was not what the natural realm could offer, but "the spiritual life in God, which is joy in the Holy Spirit." You may be wearied from your journey, as Jesus was. You need only to look to the harvest fields and find your refreshment there, in going to them with the Word of Life, for this is the food of the inner man.

> **The Holy Spirit partners with us to bring souls into the kingdom.**

We must be absorbed in God; we must live in the reality of harvest on a continual basis, as Wigglesworth did. We must live every day "with no consciousness of the world under any circumstances, except as we bring help to it." This is the refreshing! This is the sustenance of the children of God. This is the fellowship of the Holy Spirit, who partners with us to bring souls into the kingdom.

Wigglesworth, from the earliest stages of his life, found this food, this "spiritual life in God," as he described it, the continual process of leading men and women to Christ. If you want to know one of the greatest foundational truths of Wigglesworth's power in God, it was this: from the time of his salvation as a boy, he heard the heartbeat of God—which is to win souls. It became his life, his food, his drink, and eventually his constant passion, no matter where he was. He didn't turn it on and off. He didn't take a vacation from it. It wasn't his job, that he should take a rest from it, but it was the very fabric of his inner man, and it was inseparable from the life he had found as his inner man was brought to bear on everything he did. Wigglesworth's very life was sustained by doing God's bidding. His greatest delight was to win the lost for Christ.

Revival and Harvest Flow from Our Love for Christ

Revival in our lives always brings harvest. This is because the more powerful our vertical relationship is (that is, our relationship with God), the more powerful and effective our horizontal relationships will be (our relationships with others). The greater our vertical love, the greater our horizontal love. They work hand in hand. When Jesus said, *"Go therefore and make disciples of all the nations"* (Matthew 28:19), it wasn't just a recommendation or a suggestion. It was a command! It was not a law, however, but a command to be carried out through our love for Christ.

The commandments of Jesus are different from the commandments of the law. We must understand this. Jesus came to fulfill the law in us (Matthew 5:17) and to set us free from the *"curse of the law"* (Galatians 3:13), not to load us up with even more commandments, rules, and regulations. You may ask, "Why then did He give us commandments, and say, *'If anyone loves Me, he will keep My word'* (John 14:23)?"

> *The ability to obey the command of God is contained in the command itself.*

When He commanded, He commanded in accordance with the reality that He Himself came to fulfill the law, and that He is in us to fulfill it: *"Christ in you, the hope of glory"* (Colossians 1:27). This truth is reflected in another statement of Wigglesworth's. He said, "It is as easy as possible to be holy"[2] through the cross and the replacement of our life with Another's life, Another's abilities, Another's strength. It is not a question of how to obey, or if we should obey; we are only simply to obey.

Let me explain this truth still further. Jesus was not saying, "If you love Me, prove it by obeying My commandments and My words." No, that is law. Instead, the ability to obey the commandment is contained within the commandment itself. Jesus was saying, "If you love Me, you will simply find yourself obeying My commandments," for our deep love for Him brings us into oneness with Him, and we find that we have His desires, His strengths, and His abilities, and we can do nothing else but obey.

So when Jesus says, "*Go into all the world and preach the gospel to every creature*" (Mark 16:15), we find that when we deeply love Him, that is all we want to do, for it is the very "*food*" (John 4:34) and sustenance of the One within us.

> *The deeper we love Jesus, the easier it is to obey Him.*

So many messages are being preached in which the preacher tries to stir people up to go out and evangelize. There are courses, books, methods, and entire organizations dedicated to inspire people to evangelize and to train them in evangelism. However, so many of these programs end up with results like those of Acts 17:34, "*However, some men joined him and believed.*" This is because, in trying to fulfill the Great Commission, people still operate as if they are under the law instead of operating by the awesome power and wonderful grace that the commandment contains, when it is fulfilled through the cross.

The Bread from Heaven Is Yours

Friends, the "*bread from heaven*" (John 6:32) is yours. The bread is the work of the kingdom. It is the sustenance of your inner man. It is the "*hidden manna*" found in the hidden life:

> *To him who overcomes I will give some of the hidden manna to eat.* (Revelation 2:17)

> *For you died, and your life is hidden with Christ.* (Colossians 3:3)

We must find this life. There we will find the hidden manna that we long for, and we will draw men and women to the Bridegroom in multitudes.

KEY #2

POVERTY OF SPIRIT

He comes to enrapture our souls, to break every bond of mere human affection and replace in us the divine instead of the earthly, the pure instead of the unholy, the eyes of faith that see God instead of human feelings. The divine Son of God is to be in us, mightily moving through us, as we cease to be. Nothing helps us in the human place but this poverty of spirit, spoken of in this Beatitude.

We must live in such a pure atmosphere that God will shine in and through our souls. Oh, this uttermost salvation! (See Hebrews 7:25.)

"Nothing helps us in the human place but this poverty of spirit." May God bring us into the reality of being *"poor in spirit"* (Matthew 5:3). This is the primary characteristic of revival, for the more "we cease to be," the poorer in spirit we become. It is a beautiful thing to be truly poor in spirit.

Come to the Waters

Everyone who thirsts, come to the waters; and you who have no money, come, buy and eat. Yes, come, buy wine and milk without money and without price. Why do you spend money for what is not bread, and your wages for what does not satisfy? Listen carefully to Me, and eat what is good, and let your soul delight itself in abundance.

(Isaiah 55:1–2)

Let him who is thirsty come and drink. And let him who has no money come, buy, and eat. It is only the thirsty who drink from God's fountain. It is only those who truly are aware that they have nothing that is of any value to God in themselves, but are totally helpless and dependent upon Him, who ever eat the *"hidden manna"* (Revelation 2:17) from His table. For the inner man, the bride of Christ, is married to, dependent upon, and one with Christ.

When We Think We've "Got It," We've Lost It

And to the angel of the church of the Laodiceans write, "These things says the Amen, the Faithful and True Witness, the Beginning of the creation of God: 'I know your works, that you are neither cold nor hot. I could wish you were cold or hot. So then, because you are lukewarm, and neither cold nor hot, I will vomit you out of My mouth. Because you say, "I am rich, have become wealthy ["increased with goods," KJV], and have need of nothing"; and do not know that you are wretched, miserable, poor, blind, and naked; I counsel you to buy from Me gold refined in the fire, that you may be rich; and white garments, that you may be clothed, that the shame of your nakedness may not be revealed; and anoint your eyes with eye salve, that you may see. As many as I love, I rebuke and chasten. Therefore be zealous and repent. Behold, I stand at the door and knock. If anyone hears My voice and opens the door, I will come in to him and dine with him, and he with Me. To him who overcomes I will grant to sit with Me on My throne, as I also overcame and sat down with My Father on His throne. He who has an ear, let him hear what the Spirit says to the churches."' (Revelation 3:14–22)

In the church of Laodicea, we see a people rich in their own eyes; in need of nothing, according to their own opinions; *"increased with goods"* (Revelation 3:17 KJV) unto self-sufficiency and blindness. This wording is in a spiritual context; it refers to people who say, "I already know," and "I have all I need spiritually," and who don't see that this is the attitude that makes them *"wretched, miserable, poor, blind, and naked"* (Revelation 3:17).

The minute we think we've "got it," we've lost it! *"If anyone thinks that he knows anything, he knows nothing yet as he ought to know"* (1 Corinthians 8:2). The minute we think we're spiritually rich, we're poor and wretched, for we have moved back into self. The minute we are confident in our ability to see, we are blind. The minute we think we are clothed sufficiently with Him, we are naked. This is all of the natural mind, for the inner man never, ever thinks in these terms. He is *"poor in spirit"* (Matthew 5:3).

Let Your Soul Delight in His Abundance

I counsel you to buy from Me gold refined in the fire, that you may be rich; and white garments, that you may be clothed, that the shame of your nakedness may not be revealed; and anoint your eyes with eye salve, that you may see.   (Revelation 3:18)

How do we buy the gold and the garments and the eye salve? What do we have to offer God for these things? Is there anything that we can give to God to warrant our being clothed with the beautiful garment of His righteousness, *"clean and bright"* (Revelation 19:8), obtaining the wondrous treasures of heaven stored up for eternity, the *"gold refined in the fire"*? What can we possibly bring to Him? Without exception, the only thing of any value is our absolute and utter dependence on Him.

As Wigglesworth said again and again, we must come to the place of helplessness. Kathryn Kuhlman said, "My brethren, you've tried so hard....Just stop trying and surrender."[3] This is the nature of the inner

> *We must come to the place of complete helplessness, to absolute surrender.*

man. This is the nature of the bride of Christ, the one His heart longs for: She who is lost in dependence on her Bridegroom, secure only in Him. She who bears only His name, who knows no other name, and who can come in no other name. She who has no strength of her own, and who can come only in His strength.

> *Everyone who thirsts, come to the waters; and you who have no money, come, buy and eat. Yes, come, buy wine and milk without money and without price. Why do you spend money for what is not bread, and your wages for what does not satisfy? Listen carefully to Me, and eat what is good, and let your soul delight itself in abundance.* (Isaiah 55:1–2)

We are to be thirsty for Him and His love, with nothing to offer but our dependence, because we are absolutely *"poor in spirit"* (Matthew 5:3). Oh, my brothers and sisters, we've spent so much on *"what is not bread,"* we've given so much of our *"wages for what does not satisfy."*

That We Might See Him in All His Glory

He comes to enrapture our souls, to break every bond of mere human affection and exchange in us the divine for the earthly, the pure for the unholy, the eyes of faith that see God for human feelings.

He comes to bring us into the fullness of the reality of the bride of Christ within us, to "enrapture our hearts," to feed us with the bread from heaven, that wonderful hidden manna, and to serve us His *"wine and milk without money and without price"* (Isaiah 55:1). He comes to clothe us with *"fine linen, clean and bright"* (Revelation 19:8), to anoint our eyes, so that we might see Him in all His glory. All He requires is our dependence; all He desires is that we be poor in spirit. This was the very first thing He taught in the New Testament (see Matthew 5:2–3), and as it was the foundation, so it is the fulfillment of His desire for His bride.

KEY #3

THE MOURNING CRY OF THE INNER MAN

Did Jesus mean mourning over death? No, He meant mourning over our sons and daughters who have not yet touched heaven, who know nothing about the things of the Spirit of Life. When God places within us a mourning cry to move the powers of God, then He will send a revival in every home.

Paul is considered by most to be a great apostle, a great preacher, a great evangelist, and a great writer. But if we look closely at his letters, it is clear that, along with all these capacities, he was a great intercessor. By tracing his prayer life through the Epistles, we see clearly that he had this "mourning cry," and that he spent his life "mourning over the sons and daughters belonging to him, who had not yet touched heaven, and who knew nothing about the things of the Spirit of Life."

> *Therefore I also, after I heard of your faith in the Lord Jesus and your love for all the saints, do not cease to give thanks for you, making mention of you in my prayers.* (Ephesians 1:15–16)

> *For this reason I bow my knees to the Father of our Lord Jesus Christ, from whom the whole family in heaven and earth is named, that He would grant you, according to the riches of His glory, to be strengthened with might through His Spirit in the inner man.* (Ephesians 3:14–16)

In the quote at the beginning of this section, Wigglesworth was primarily speaking of natural families and natural sons and daughters, and we must apply this truth to our families. However, I have also referred to Paul here and included the verses from Ephesians because he is a classic example for us in this regard. He considered all those who had believed through his preaching to be his own sons and daughters, and his inner man mourned over them, so that he cried, *"My little children, for whom I labor in birth again until Christ is formed in you"* (Galatians 4:19). He interceded and travailed on their behalf so that they might "touch heaven" and come to know "the things of the Spirit of Life."

> **God will send revival into every home in answer to our mourning cries.**

It is impossible to get this spiritual mourning over lost souls without having the very next thing that God says, "[You] *shall be comforted.*" As though God could give you a spirit of mourning over a needy soul, and then not give you victory! Beloved, it is the mighty power of God in us. And when the Spirit brings us to this mourning attitude over lost souls and over all the failures that we see in professing Christians, until we can go into the presence of God with that mourning spirit, nothing will happen. But when that happens, rejoice; God will bring you through.

God wants us to rejoice today. He has brought us into this blessed place so that we may mourn and then rejoice.

It is in this "blessed place" that we must live. It is the hidden place, the "*secret place*" (Psalm 91:1). It is the reality of Colossians 3:3: "*For you died, and your life is hidden with Christ in God.*" It is the place that every revivalist who has walked the earth lived in. And the only way into it is through the cross. Until we see it and live in it, "nothing will happen." But, "beloved, it is the mighty power of God in us. And when the Spirit brings us to this mourning attitude over lost souls and over all the failures that we see in professing Christians," when we are living fully as the new man, "when that happens, rejoice; God will bring you through. God wants us to rejoice today. He has brought us into this blessed place so that we may mourn and then rejoice."

KEY #4

RIGHTEOUSNESS IS A WALK WITH GOD

But the height of divine touches of heaven never leaves you stationary but rather increases your thirst and appetite for greater things. Something within makes you press on until you are empty of everything else so that you may be filled with what God is pressing in. This righteousness is a walk with God. It is a divine inheritance. It is seeing the face of Jesus until you cannot be satisfied without drinking of His Spirit and being overflowed continually with His blessings. I cannot be satisfied without Christ's righteousness.

We are caught today in a dilemma. We teach the truth in our churches, but our emphasis on biblical head knowledge to the neglect of heart response can leave Christians very much in a "stationary" place, as Wigglesworth referred to, self-satisfied with their spiritual state and not dependent on God. Consequently, we never really come into this place of "thirst and appetite for greater things," the "something within that makes you press on until you are empty of everything else so that you may be filled with what God is pressing in." This leaves us without "the height of divine touches of heaven" and, ultimately, we end up in the condition of the church of the Laodiceans.

The Outworking of Righteousness in Our Daily Lives

If I were to say to you, "You must hunger and thirst for righteousness with all your heart," perhaps you would answer, "I am the righteousness of God in Christ Jesus" (see 2 Corinthians 5:21), to which I would emphatically agree. You are the righteousness of God. But we must declare that we are the righteousness of God in our inner man, and this hunger and thirst for righteousness must consume us so that the power of the righteousness within us may come forth in our day-to-day, outward walk.

The positional teaching of who we are in Christ, which I spoke about in the first section of this book, has done wonders for so many in the body of Christ over the past fifty years. However, because it has not been balanced with teaching about the cross, it has also left multitudes living in mediocrity and denial, sitting content and stationary in a "positional" righteousness

> *Righteousness that is a walk with God will exhibit itself powerfully in our lives.*

without having any real outworking, or manifestation, of its power in their lives.

Wigglesworth was clearly speaking of righteousness that is "worked out," or manifested powerfully, in our lives, when he said, "This righteousness is a walk with God." There are so many Christians who have lost their "hunger and thirst for greater things," who have become truly blinded to their need of outworked righteousness and to the reality of their wretched state, because of a false security built on false faith. True faith will bring about its object. False faith absolutely will not. It will simply lull us into complacency.

Wigglesworth was called "The Apostle of Faith," and he is being used by many Christian leaders today as an example in their teaching to illustrate the principles of faith they wish to convey. Unfortunately, many take from Wiggles-worth what fits their favorite concepts, and they leave out the essential foundations that God was teaching us through him. In fact, Wigglesworth rarely taught faith "principles," but rather, as Louis Pethrus said, "inoculated" people with God's kind of faith, which does not flow from principles but from a deep relationship with Him. Faith principles will ultimately fail and leave us perplexed and dismayed unless we have the outworking of the message of the cross in our lives.

You Can Be an Instrument of Revival

> *Faith principles will fail unless we have the manifestation of the cross in our lives.*

When you see all the fullness of God's Word through the cross, you will have the "mourning cry." You will come to the depths of God as Wigglesworth knew them. You will see your need for outworked righteousness. You will see how wretched your natural thinking and "old man" actually are. You will come to lose your own life and find the beauty of the "divine inheritance of seeing the face of Jesus until you cannot be satisfied without drinking of His Spirit and being overflowed with His blessings."

You will become an instrument of revival.

KEY #5

REVIVAL IN ME

I used to have such a bad temper that it made me tremble all over. It would make me furious with its evil power. I saw that this temper had to be destroyed; it could not be patched up. One day the power of God fell upon me. I came to the meeting and fell down before the Lord. The people began asking, "What sin has Wigglesworth been committing?" This went on for two weeks. Every time I came to the altar, God used to sweep through me with such a manifestation of my helplessness that I would go down before God and weep right through. Then the preacher or the leader would be broken up and come beside me. God started a revival that way. God had broken me up, and revival began through His revival in me.

When God has likewise "broken us up," revival will begin in us. God is looking for more Wigglesworths, Finneys, Whitefields, and Kuhlmans! He is looking for men and women who will hunger after Him and fall down before Him until He "sweeps through them with such a manifestation of their helplessness" that they become pure channels of His power.

Become a "Flame of Fire"

I pray that this little book has lit a fire—a "magnificent passion"—in you and that your life will never be the same! May it lead you to the altar again and again, like Wigglesworth, even while others around you are saying, "What sin has he been committing?" And may you stay there until God "sweeps through you with such a manifestation

> *Press into God until you become a bright "flame of fire" in the kingdom.*

of your helplessness that you will go down before the Lord and weep right through." I pray that other preachers and leaders will come alongside you, and that, as with Wigglesworth, God will "start a revival that way." May you press in until you become a *"flame of fire"* (Psalm 104:4), a revivalist in your own part of the world.

I also pray that you will come to know, as Wigglesworth did, that God has "no other plan for the baptized soul except to be *'dead indeed to sin'* (Romans 6:11)," that you will become one of the grains of wheat that falls to the ground and dies, so that you will produce much fruit for God. (See John 12:24.) May you be a soldier in the great end-times revival!

EPILOGUE:

KATHRYN KUHLMAN
TESTIMONY

I conclude with an amazing testimony from more recent times, that of evangelist Kathryn Kuhlman. When I first heard this testimony on cassette tape, I sat and wept. She spoke the very same message of the cross and revival with such a clarity and authority that it provides the perfect conclusion to this book. I share it here so that you might see again this great secret of revival from the testimony of another twentieth-century revivalist. I have retained the original phrasing and flavor of her spoken message.

One day, I shall never forget it as long as I live, I had a sorrow, I had a heartbreak. A late Saturday afternoon, walking down a dead-end street, and literally, it was a dead-end street. I can go to the very place. I can go to the very spot. Alone. Looking up, I shall never—.

Beloved, these things are as real to me this moment as the hour when they happened. In that moment, knowing nothing about the fullness of the Holy Spirit—. Everything I know, He has taught me—everything, believe me. Four o'clock that Saturday afternoon, having come to the place in my life where I surrendered. I knew nothing about the fullness of the Holy Spirit. I knew nothing about the baptism in the Holy Spirit. I knew nothing about speaking in an unknown tongue. I knew nothing about the deeper truths of the Word. All that I knew was that I loved souls. That's all that I knew! Souls, souls, souls! I only knew that a person would be lost if he did not accept Christ as his Savior, that's all that I knew.

In that moment, with the tears streaming down my face, then looking up and vowing, He and I made each other promises. There are some things that you don't talk about. There are some things that are so sacred, you just don't talk about those things. There are just some things that are terrifically personal between the two of you. It's like some things that are just so personal between a husband and wife, you just don't display them out in public. He knows that I'll be true to Him as long as my old heart will keep beating. And I know that I'll be true to Him. We have a pact, and it's all settled.

At the end of a dead-end street, four o'clock on Saturday afternoon—in that moment when I yielded to Him body, soul, and spirit, when I gave Him everything, all there was of me, I knew then, beloved, what the Scripture meant, and you'll never change the meaning of it: "If any man will follow Me, let him take up his cross." (See Matthew 16:24.) Beloved, the cross is always the sign, the symbol, of death. It's the symbol of death! That afternoon, "Kathryn Kuhlman" died. I mean died! Kathryn Kuhlman died!

If I were to tell you that I don't even associate that name with myself—. I tell you the truth, I died. If you've never had that death to the flesh, you don't know what I'm talking—. There's some of you who know.

When it comes to the baptism in the Holy Spirit, I know what I believe, and you'll never change my mind; I know. Nobody believes in the baptism in the Holy Spirit, nobody believes in the fullness of the Holy Spirit, call it what you will, nobody believes in it more than Kathryn Kuhlman. I know; I have experienced it. I have experienced the baptism in the Holy Spirit, and I want it to go on record.

You want to know whether I'm Pentecostal? I'm more Pentecostal than the most Pentecostal person who claims to be Pentecostal today. I believe in it, as it was in the early church. I do not believe in a lot of fanaticism; I do not believe in the manifestation of the flesh, but beloved, I am going to tell you something: I believe in the speaking in an unknown tongue, but there are still people today who speak with an unknown tongue who have never been baptized in the Holy Spirit!

When you are completely filled with the Holy Spirit, my friends, when you are baptized in the Holy Spirit, when you have had that experience that they had in the Upper Room, there will be a crucifying of the flesh. There will be a death of the flesh, believe me. You will die! You will die! And there are a lot of professing Christians, professing to being filled with the Holy Spirit, who have never died to the flesh. You know something, that's the reason that Scripture I read you describes me perfectly: *"For ye see your calling, brethren, how that not many wise men after the flesh, not many mighty, not many noble, are called: but God hath chosen the foolish things of the world to confound the wise; and God hath chosen the weak things of the world to confound the things which are mighty"* (1 Corinthians 1:26–27 KJV). Nothing—He doesn't ask for golden vessels. No, had He wanted any of these, He wouldn't have chosen that redheaded, mean, little, freckled-face girl in Missouri. All He needs is somebody that will die! Somebody who'll die! And when I died, He came in; I was baptized, I was filled with His Spirit, I spoke in an unknown tongue, as He took every part of me. In that moment, I surrendered unto Him all there was of me! Everything! Everything! Then, for the first time, I realized what it meant to have power.

You know, we talk about miracles. We've gotten so that the word *miracles* is on the lips of thousands of people. We don't have to pray for miracles when we get in the position—where the two meet, you see the result of that meeting, and there'll automatically be miracles. It's something that you don't work up.

I started to preach on the Holy Spirit; He was so real to me. The Holy Spirit people: please let me just pause and say something. Oh, I'm so sold on the Holy Spirit. Don't you understand, people? Without the Holy Spirit, I'm sunk; I haven't a crutch, I haven't anything, to lean on. I don't have a thing! You see, if I'd been born with talent, I might have been able to lean on that; had I had education, I might have used that as a crutch, but I don't have a thing. I don't have a thing! I don't have a crutch; I don't have a thing to lean on. Nothing! That's what He said. He'd take the base things, the most unlikely things. Why? So that He might receive the glory. I'm so sold on the Holy Spirit because I know that without the power of the Holy Spirit, I don't have a thing; I'm sunk.

Do you want me to bear my soul? I'll bear my soul to you: in these great miracle services, before I walk from behind the wings and come out on that stage, I die a thousand deaths. The longest walk that I ever take is the walk from behind the wings, behind the curtains, and stand behind the pulpit, wherever it is, because I know better than anyone else that I have nothing. Absolutely nothing! Nobody in the whole world knows it better than I do. I die a thousand deaths when I take that walk! I may smile, and sometimes think that I walk so fast because I can hardly wait for that anointing to come upon me. I know that out there, when I face that crowd and I stand there, that there are those people that are out there, some having made great sacrifices to come. There's cancer out there; somebody's last hope. I'm so conscious of it; I'm so aware of it. And I know that I can't give it to them; I know that I don't have any healing virtue. People, I don't have any virtue; I don't have any healing power, please believe me. Believe me! Without the power of the Holy Ghost, I'm sunk.

And you talk about the gifts of the Spirit, believe me—. Hear the truth, I have never, and I'll live or die and no one will ever hear Kathryn Kuhlman boast of any of the gifts. And I believe in the gifts. O my brethren, my precious sisters in the Lord, I believe in the gifts of the Spirit. I believe in the gifts with every atom of my being! In fact, I believe so much in the gifts of the Holy Spirit that I do not believe in limiting the Holy Spirit to just nine gifts of the Spirit. I believe that there are many more than just the nine. Don't limit Him; don't limit Him, whatever you do! I believe, beloved, not only in the baptism in the Holy Spirit, I believe that we should see the gifts of the Spirit in operation in every church in America! And I believe that the nearer we come to the closing of this dispensation, we're going to see—.

Get ready, what I'm talking to you about today is the most up-to-date thing that I could talk to you about! We are living in the closing moments of this dispensation. I'm talking to you about something that's vitally important, and I pray that out of this session and out of this hour of speaking, the Holy Spirit shall call men and women that He can use, who are willing to die to self.

I believe, beloved, in the gifts of the Spirit, and the operation of the gifts, and I also believe that if one has received a gift, or any number of gifts, he'll not go around boasting about it. I get scared sick when somebody comes in front of me and says, "Miss Kuhlman, I have the gift of so-and-so." I get scared. You see, there's something about the Holy Spirit—. I had an experience several weeks ago, a Jewish gentleman who had just found Christ as the great Messiah. I was alone with him in a chapel. I saw a man, I heard a man, worship God!

Sometimes I think you and I get too familiar with God. Don't misconstrue what I've just said; please do not. Sometimes I think we get too familiar with Him. He's a holy God; He's a holy God! About Jesus, oh, the power there is, in even His name! The name of Jesus. Jesus. Sometimes I think we become too familiar with the Holy Spirit. I can only tell you of my relationship with Him, that's all. He's so wonderful. Do you realize He is the power of the Trinity? He's as real to me as any human being who exists this hour.

I live a very lonely life. When I'm not in the crowds, I'm alone. He's all that I have. I've learned to follow Him. He isn't a person that I can use. You know, we've tried to use the Holy Spirit for so long. We've tried to use Him, and we've gotten into trouble. That's the reason some of our testimonies are so empty, so without power. That's the reason we've gone off in the flesh. Have you really gotten acquainted with Him? Really? When you really love someone, you want to know their disposition, their likes and their dislikes. Do you really know Him? Do you know Him as a person? Not just in having spoken in tongues. I'm talking about really knowing a person. I would not dare boast of having any gift, because after all is said and done, it's still the Holy Spirit using the empty vessel. It's still the Holy Spirit; it's still the person. All I have to do is furnish the vessel. That's all… that's all…that's all. My brethren, you've tried so hard. You've struggled and you've strained. And you've agonized and you've sought. Little lady, you've tried, tried so hard. Just stop trying and surrender.[1]

END NOTES

Editor's Note: The biographical information and miraculous events of Smith Wigglesworth's ministry have been recorded by several authors. In cases where information has not been directly quoted, the citations below are the most complete or primary sources found for the particular topic.

Introduction: The Legacy of Smith Wigglesworth

[1] Adapted from Albert Hibbert, *Smith Wigglesworth: The Secret of His Power* (Tulsa, OK: Harrison House, 1993), 69–70.

[2] Adapted from Albert Hibbert, *The Secret of His Power* (Tulsa, OK: Harrison House, 1993), 28, and Stanley H. Frodsham, *Smith Wigglesworth: Apostle of Faith* (Springfield, MO: Gospel Publishing House, 1993), 103.

[3] Adapted from Smith Wigglesworth, "Life in the Spirit," sermon, originally published in *The Pentecostal Evangel*.

[4] See Peter Madden, *The Wigglesworth Standard* (New Kensington, PA: Whitaker House, 1993).

[5] Madden, *The Wigglesworth Standard*, 195.

Part 1: Passing the Mantle

[1] Albert Hibbert, *Smith Wigglesworth: The Secret of His Power* (Tulsa, OK: Harrison House, 1993), 59.

[2] Hibbert, *The Secret of His Power*, 14.

[3] Ibid.

[4] Hibbert, *The Secret of His Power*, 14–15.

[5] Madden, *The Wigglesworth Standard* (New Kensington, PA: Whitaker House, 1993), 7.

[6] George Stormont, *Wigglesworth: A Man Who Walked with God* (Tulsa: Harrison House, 1989), 9.

Part 2: Epistles of Christ

Smith Wigglesworth's sermon, "Epistles of Christ: Manifesting Forth His Glory," was originally published in *Triumphs of Faith* and is used courtesy of the Home of Peace, Oakland, California.

[1] William Hacking, *Smith Wigglesworth Remembered* (Tulsa, OK: Harrison House, 1982), 74.

[2] Hibbert, *The Secret of His Power*, 10.

[3] Harold A. Fischer, *Reviving Revivals*, 78, quoted in Winkie Pratney, *Revival* (Springdale, PA: Whitaker House, 1984), 25.

[4] Fischer, *Reviving Revivals*, 84–86, quoted in Pratney, *Revival*, 26.

[5] J. [John] C. [Charles] Ryle, *Christian Leaders of the Eighteenth Century*, 49, quoted in Pratney, *Revival*, 98.

[6] See Ryle, *Christian Leaders of the Eighteenth Century*, 39, quoted in Pratney, *Revival*, 101.

[7] George Whitefield, *Journals*, 223, quoted in Pratney, *Revival*, 102.

[8] Pratney, *Revival*, 102.

[9] Ryle, *Christian Leaders*, 52, quoted in Pratney, *Revival*, 99.

[10] Ryle, *Christian Leaders*, 54, quoted in Pratney, *Revival*, 100.

[11] Ibid.

[12] Ibid.

[13] Pratney, *Revival*, 109.

[14] Fischer, *Reviving Revivals*, 156, quoted in Pratney, *Revival*, 112.

[15] From the cover jacket of Charles G. Finney by Basil Miller, quoted in Pratney, *Revival*, 127.

[16] Smith Wigglesworth, "Like Precious Faith," sermon, originally published in *Triumphs of Faith*, used courtesy of the Home of Peace, Oakland, California.

[17] Madden, *The Wigglesworth Standard*, 29.

[18] Friend, conversation with author, Sonora, California, September 1993.

[19] Pratney, *Revival*, 128–134. Note: Pratney's quotation from Finney's *Systematic Theology* is taken from J. H. Fairchild, ed., *Finney's Systematic Theology* (Bethany Fellowship, 1976). Pratney's quotations from Finney's autobiography are taken from Helen Wessel, ed., *The Autobiography of Charles Finney*, (Bethany Fellowship, 1977).

[20] Pratney, *Revival*, 96–98.

[21] Madden, *The Wigglesworth Standard*, 47.

[22] "Until That Final Day" by Keith Green. Birdwing Music/BMG Songs, Inc./Ears to Hear Music. All rights reserved. Used by permission.

[23] "My Eyes Are Dry" by Keith Green. Birdwing Music/BMG Songs, Inc./Ears to Hear Music. All rights reserved. Used by permission.

[24] This pamphlet has been reprinted under the title "Keith Green: The Man Behind the Message" by Last Days Ministries, P. O. Box 40, Lindale, Texas 75771.

Part 3: Uttermost Salvation

Smith Wigglesworth's sermon, "Uttermost Salvation," was originally published in *Triumphs of Faith* and is used courtesy of the Home of Peace, Oakland, California.

[1] Evangelist Ray Bloomfield, conversation with author, Brisbane, Australia, August 1996.

[2] Smith Wigglesworth, "Changed from Glory to Glory," sermon, originally published in *Triumphs of Faith*, used courtesy of the Home of Peace, Oakland, California.

[3] Used by permission. The Kathryn Kuhlman Foundation, Pittsburgh, Pennsylvania.

Epilogue: Kathryn Kuhlman Testimony

[1] Used by permission. The Kathryn Kuhlman Foundation, Pittsburgh, Pennsylvania.

SUGGESTED READING

Books about Smith Wigglesworth:

Frodsham, Stanley Howard. *Smith Wigglesworth: Apostle of Faith.* Springfield, MO: Gospel Publishing House, 1990.

Hacking, W. [William]. *Smith Wigglesworth Remembered.* Tulsa, OK: Harrison House, 1981.

Hibbert, Albert. *Smith Wigglesworth: The Secret of His Power.* Tulsa, OK: Harrison House, 1993.

Madden, Peter. *The Wigglesworth Standard.* New Kensington, PA: Whitaker House, 1993.

Stormont, George. *Wigglesworth: A Man Who Walked with God.* Tulsa, OK: Harrison House, 1989.

BOOKS ON REVIVAL:

Buckingham, Jamie. *Daughter of Destiny.* North Brunswick, NJ: Bridge-Logos Publishers, 1987.

Nee, Watchman. *Release of the Spirit.* Fort Washington, PA: Christian Literature Crusade, 1989.

Pratney, Winkie. *Revival.* Springdale, PA: Whitaker House, 1984.

ABOUT THE AUTHOR

PETER J. MADDEN

For over two decades, Peter J. Madden has served as pastor, evangelist, camp and conference speaker, and worship leader. After pioneering churches in both Australia and the United States, he now travels internationally, preaching the message of the cross in crusades, conferences, and churches throughout Asia, Europe, America, and Africa.

Peter was born in 1961 in Sydney, Australia. His interest in evangelist Smith Wigglesworth was sparked when he first heard Wigglesworth's name, and the Holy Spirit instructed him that he was to go and learn about the great evangelist. In 1989, after pastoring a church in Wollongong, Australia, he and his family traveled to California and were led by God to an old missionary home in Oakland where many great men and women of the faith had stayed in years past. It was there, in an old cupboard in the front room of the house, that he discovered thirty-seven of Smith Wigglesworth's messages. These sermons are the basis for both this book and his first book, *The Wigglesworth Standard*, which has sold over 100,000 copies (also published by Whitaker House).

He has established Flames of Fire Ministries to help others kindle the same kind of fire and commitment to God that Wigglesworth and other great revivalists had, so that they also may glorify God and serve others powerfully in the love of Christ.

Peter J. Madden
Flames of Fire Ministries
P.O. Box 3663
Robina, T.C., Queensland, Australia 4230